Sharing Profits

Also by John N. Reynolds

ETHICS IN INVESTMENT BANKING *(with Edmund Newell)*

Sharing Profits

The Ethics of Remuneration, Tax and Shareholder Returns

John N. Reynolds

Softcover reprint of the hardcover 1st edition 2015 978-1-137-44544-5

First published 2015 by
PALGRAVE MACMILLAN

Palgrave Macmillan in the UK is an imprint of Macmillan Publishers Limited,
registered in England, company number 785998, of Houndmills, Basingstoke,
Hampshire RG21 6XS.

Palgrave Macmillan in the US is a division of St Martin's Press LLC,
175 Fifth Avenue, New York, NY 10010.

Palgrave Macmillan is the global academic imprint of the above companies
and has companies and representatives throughout the world.

Palgrave® and Macmillan® are registered trademarks in the United States,
the United Kingdom, Europe and other countries

ISBN 978-1-349-49578-8   ISBN 978-1-137-44545-2 (eBook)
DOI 10.1057/9781137445452

This book is printed on paper suitable for recycling and made from fully
managed and sustained forest sources. Logging, pulping and manufacturing
processes are expected to conform to the environmental regulations of the
country of origin.

A catalogue record for this book is available from the British Library.

A catalog record for this book is available from the Library of Congress.

Transferred to Digital Printing in 2015

For Karen

Contents

Acknowledgements

This book is possible because of the experience I gained from being able to be a part of the Church of England Ethical Investment Advisory Group, and the Central Finance Board of the Methodist Church. I thank Richard Burridge, Claire Foster, Edmund Newell and Peter Selby for their efforts to educate me about applied ethics. I am indebted to Ed Newell for his assistance and advice, and to Claire Foster who was responsible for my use of a rights-based, duty-based structure. Bill Seddon, Stephen Beer, William Eason, Roger Reynolds, Mark Rosenberg, Dominic Tayler, Alex Turnbull, Simon Oakland and Richard Moore have all provided me with insights from fund managers and investment bankers. David Gray and Alan Sutherland have helped me understand in better detail regulation, and the interaction of government and business. Stephen Green and Philip Hampton have helped with understanding deliberations on remuneration. Deborah Sabalot has continued to keep me informed about regulatory law and provided excellent advice in discussing a number of detailed questions. The support I received at the EIAG from Neville White, Amanda Young and Edward Mason was superb, and the EIAG could not have functioned without them.

I gratefully acknowledge this expert help, but must accept sole responsibility for any errors, and for my views, conclusions and the inevitable baggage I carry with me.

I know you won't all agree with much of this book given how contentious the subject matter can be, but if you have read it, and it has made you think, thank you.

1
Introduction and Summary

> *Nothing is beneficial that is not also honourable, and nothing is honourable that is not also beneficial... no greater plague has assailed human life than the fancy of those who have separated the two.*

> Marcus Tullius Cicero, *On Duties*

- Any decision regarding tax, remuneration or shareholder *returns* has ethical implications.
- Standards of *business ethics* are disappointing and need addressing in order to preserve shareholder value – but these standards reflect ethical issues throughout society.
- Executive remuneration is complex because there is no obvious single correct level or structure.
- A poor CEO can destroy many times more value than their remuneration. Insufficient executive remuneration can create risks for shareholders and companies.
- However, shareholders often feel unrepresented in the negotiation of executive remuneration, with unjustified levels negotiated supposedly on their behalf. While supportive of proper remuneration for the successful executive, there are concerns over instances of an unjustified transfer of shareholder value to executives, notably in the case of payments for failure. An increasing proportion of equity in remuneration will lead in some cases to higher rewards, but in general will also create more disparate outcomes.

1

- Governments have failed to adapt legislation to match the business environment, notably with regard to the internet and globalisation – using tax as a source of comparative advantage while simultaneously excoriating companies for tax avoidance.
- Businesses and governments are somewhere in the middle of a major process of change in the commercial, financial and political environment. This change in environment has seen a reduction in corporate taxes, and the process of tax reduction may continue, under the pressure of competition in tax rates to attract business, to a minimum level to maintain stability and educate and care for skilled workers. This may challenge aspirations for the welfare state in countries which are not resource rich, notably in northern Europe.
- There have been numerous instances of ethical failings by major companies and the popular conception of company behaviour is often poor.
- Even though ethical principles are difficult to translate into numbers, much of the theory and practice of capital and investment allocation are closely correlated with key ethical principles: notably equality and justice.
- Shareholders are ethically entitled to earn an appropriate risk-adjusted return on investment, provided they do not breach duties to other groups – but these duties need to be understood and accepted. Companies and shareholders benefit from the stability provided by government, especially from limitations on liability. This places a clear ethical obligation on companies.
- Companies cannot effectively address social problems and government policy ambitions themselves, such as addressing income inequality – pushing the onus onto business is occasionally justified, but much more often unjustified, and has to remain with government. The most commonly recognised symbols of income inequality in many deprived areas are often associated with the drugs trade and with celebrities, not with highly paid executives.
- Companies need to adopt clear prioritised ethical frameworks of rights and duties to make informed decisions on how profits are used, and to be transparent about what values are used and how they are implemented.
- In many cases, applying an ethical framework is more likely to help define *how* a decision should be implemented, rather than necessarily changing the decision. To be meaningful, any ethical

framework has to take into account the actions and activities contemplated.

Any decision regarding tax, remuneration or shareholder returns has ethical implications. It is no longer sufficient just to be legal. The unethical today has a risk and a cost in the future. A company, and more precisely its directors, have a duty to its shareholders to maximise its value. It also has duties to other constituencies: to its clients or customers, to its creditors, suppliers and other contractual counterparties, to the government or governments of countries in which it operates, to its employees. Balancing the primary duty to shareholders against other responsibilities is not straightforward. Neither is it purely a financial issue, as decisions have long-term implications (which in turn can impact value). Even from the perspective that the duty to shareholders takes priority above all others, it is important to understand that these duties include managing the risk of harm to shareholder value which could result from causing damage to other groups – such as local communities and employees – and a framework to consider such issues is essential to preserve long-term shareholder value.

The combination of the internet age and globalisation have fundamentally changed the relationship between government and the multinational company. Legislators, governments and international bodies are struggling vainly to catch up. This has profound implications for companies and individuals. Governments are finding difficulty articulating and coping with the resulting challenges, which will fundamentally change the interaction between government and company. Just as the internet changed Main Street/High Street/HauptStrasse before government policy could be adjusted to maintain city centres, so the changes in company structure will threaten the competitiveness and ultimately the survival of longstanding business sectors if governments do not change their attitude to dealing with them.

Managing the relationship and share of profits between shareholders, employees and the state can be complex, and to be done on a clear and informed basis consideration needs to include stated and *prioritised* ethical rules:

- Shareholders provide capital to businesses, and it is reasonable that they should do so in the expectation that they should be able to earn a reasonable return. There is no large-scale, realistic, alternative model to manage investment and capital allocation for the benefit of society.

- Companies have difficulty in determining how much decision making to refer to shareholders. Although companies may frequently pay insufficient regard to shareholders, at the same time in a major company decision making can be remarkably complex, and even non-executive directors may now find themselves working close to full time.
- It is largely correct to say that the private sector – individual companies and those employed by private companies – fund government.
- In many cases, companies can operate either directly because of government, notably benefiting from "limited liability" on their shareholders and directors, or because they are licensed to extract minerals for example. Government provides stability and services essential to business, such as education.
- Companies have a corresponding duty to support governments. However, the pressure on governments, especially in a democracy, is to appeal to the popular vote. As a result, governments may say one thing, while the impact of their legislation knowingly does something different. In dealing with the state, companies need to – and do – interpret what governments want to see, but at the same time they are aware that the life expectancy of a major company goes beyond normal election cycles.
- Companies have a longer vision than the term of office of many governments. A company's ethical duties will therefore correspond to supporting government in general, but generally not equate to party political activity.
- The remuneration of executives – especially of a CEO – needs to be relevant to the role, and not risk transferring value at the expense of shareholders. The state is not *directly* at risk from high remuneration, as personal taxes now generally exceed corporate tax rates, as a largely unacknowledged impact of globalisation.
- Use of ethical codes can be meaningful in both reaching and communicating decisions. Ethics is not so good for providing actual numbers (which ethical groups should accept can be a bit of a limitation regarding issues such as remuneration). These codes need to recognise the most important ethical rights and duties pertaining to a company, and be clear regarding the hierarchy or prioritisation associated with these rules.

There has been widespread and probably increasingly vocal criticism of aspects of corporate behaviour: the remuneration of executives, especially in banking has led to much criticism and in some cases clear shareholder revolts. Credit Suisse pleaded guilty to charges associated with "an extensive and wide-ranging conspiracy to help US taxpayers evade taxes,"[1] agreeing to pay $1.8 billion in fines and restitutions. The tax paid (or not) by various multinational companies has been excoriated by the UK's Public Accounts Committee. It is important to understand that criticism of tax arrangements is levelled at both new economy companies (such as Google), and old economy (such as Starbucks – coffee shops are a very longstanding form of activity). Despite an unprecedentedly sophisticated and complex remuneration report, a number of investors have either publicly or through voting at its 2014 AGM shown their unwillingness to support incentive pay arrangements within Barclays, a UK-based banking group. Barclays' incentive pay or bonus pool (to a large group of employees) exceeds dividend payments, which brings into sharp focus both the question of how profits are shared, and how bankers are paid. Specifically, this highlights the difficulty faced by a Board considering a need to invest in mobile intellectual capital, in the form of talented employees, or risk a loss in value, at a time where shareholder returns are modest.

Tax, dividends and bonuses are all paid out of the same pot of money – the profits earned by a company. Companies making decisions regarding one of these payments are by definition affecting the other two. And the interaction between these payments can be surprising, even counter-intuitive. For example, and perhaps ironically, with (much) higher taxes on pay than on corporate profits, the tax authorities are likely to actually lose revenue from lower bonus payments. Tax can be used as one of a number of explicit incentives by governments, including to persuade companies to locate in one particular area (or to relocate from one area to another).

There is a gulf between political posturing and political action, partly reflecting hard economic realities – governments actually need successful companies in order to make their states work financially and socially. It is all well and good to "render unto Caesar,"[2] but for an international company the competing demands from different tax jurisdictions can equate to more than a company's entire profits, which rather necessitates an informed debate between the company and the tax authorities, and why can't Caesar tell us a bit more simply how much he actually wants?

Tax law and international co-operation on tax has struggled unsurprisingly to keep pace with changes resulting from the move of commerce onto the internet, with profound consequences for day-to-day lives, as well as to business models. There is an obligation on governments to maintain tax *regulations* fairly and consistently. This is difficult, and manifestly an area which is currently problematic, giving rise to some of the problems causing companies to struggle with decisions today. On its own, blaming companies for difficulty in determining how to respond to the inconsistency between tax law and business models is not a fair way for tax authorities to handle this situation. Geopolitics and global trade have changed rapidly in the internet age, and will continue to change, in ways which are unpredictable. The free movement of capital, intellectual property and scope to move operations has contributed to a change in approach in corporation tax. The evolution of taxation may change further, pushing higher burdens on personal taxes, or reducing welfare payments. Companies need to take into account the long-term implications of such pressures for change and the resulting changes, and a conscious ethical dimension to decision making helps protect against decisions which are strictly legal today being seen as actively immoral tomorrow.

Much should and can be done by companies to resolve ethical problems themselves. Ultimately, any attempt to improve the ethical standards of a company, or across business more generally, will only succeed if it is based on inculcating standards across a whole company. Creation of governance committees, more attention on ethics by Boards, more comprehensive codes of conduct, will in the end fail if they do not go throughout the company.

In researching this book, it became clear very quickly that there is widespread cynicism about the motivation of executives, including from groups which would be expected to support them: shareholders and non-executive directors and even Chairmen of major companies. Given this widespread view, there are two different conclusions which could be arrived at: first, that there should be a radical change, or second, that there is no easy radical change. Given that the tendency of investors in large *private* companies is to offer high rewards, and that high rewards are paid to leading actors, musicians, politicians and lottery winners, it seems difficult to conclude that structures for remunerating executives in quoted companies are simply "broken" rather than being imperfect just because they can result in very high remuneration. In fact, one of the supposed "solutions" to the incentives on banking executives, a group which contributed to the financial crisis, is to pay higher proportions of remuneration in the form of shares. This in itself, in a successful company, will lead to remuneration being higher rather than lower. It will also lead to a randomness in ultimate rewards, with a higher level of divergence in the actual remuneration of executives.

Corporate understanding of ethics is poor, and often left to Board committees, or outside advisers (legal or accounting). Even those organisations attempting to address ethical questions seem sometimes to start from startling positions of ignorance. Advertisements for major companies and public sector institutions seeking to recruit specialists in business ethics highlight the lack of corporate understanding of what ethics is really about: stipulating a background specifically in law or HR without requiring the study of ethics *per se* seems to be pretty daft (it's difficult to imagine the reverse situation). Companies seem readily to revert to a consequentialist or *utilitarian* defence of decisions when they apply ethical thinking: "We would do it more responsibly than others." The problem with this approach is that it can be used to defend almost any behaviour and does not stand up to much scrutiny.

Shareholders often justifiably feel unrepresented in a negotiation of executive remuneration. Shareholder consultation in many cases needs to be more meaningful. Remuneration Committees need to be seen to be following what is already good practice, by taking shareholder concerns seriously, rather than meeting major shareholders primarily to explain. If points of comparison outside quoted companies are used to justify the remuneration of executives, they will not be convincing when they are only based on highly remunerated sectors (such as *Private Equity*), while ignoring much lower remunerated sectors (such as NGOs).

Ethical standards in business reflect ethical standards in society as a whole. Political and media criticism of business is not unbiased. Politicians in democracies seek to sway voters, and statements on corporate behaviour are not reflected in political actions. Media criticism needs to be understood in context – much of media is about numbers of readers, viewers, likes and other indicators of influence.

The hyperbole from some critics does not help the debate, but the cavalier attitude of some companies (albeit a minority) hardens attitudes against corporate behaviour. Globalisation, as Stephen Green observes in *Good Value*,[3] is a phenomenon, and is not a conspiracy. The lag in governments adjusting regulation, tax and law to deal with both globalisation and the internet should not be a surprise, but at the same time needs to be acknowledged as a contributing factor to the confusion in understanding how companies should conduct themselves.

There are partial solutions to the problems identified. These include companies taking on Boards' codes of ethics propagated throughout their workforce, as well as Boards consciously taking into account ethical issues when deciding on remuneration, dividends and tax, and not just applying ethical thinking as (i) an afterthought, (ii) a tick-box *compliance* exercise or (iii) a parallel exercise to actual decision making.

Ethical debate about issues such as tax and remuneration is intense, and often leads to irreconcilable differences between two different approaches: ethical traditions deriving concepts of duty and virtue set out by Aristotle and Plato and developed by St Augustine, Aquinas and Kant place a clear focus on freedom; whereas much recent ethical thinking and commentary challenges the limitations for freedom as resulting in a lack of justice or fairness. Ultimately, the underlying premises behind these different schools of thought are likely to prove irreconcilable: if high remuneration is deemed to be unethical *per se*, as a Kantian *categorical imperative*, then "free bargaining" must have clear limits. This may seem attractive at first – but who sets these limits, how, and how can this apply to business without applying to actors and sports stars? It is difficult to get away from the influence of envy on discussing limits to remuneration if the limits are not set by the Board and its shareholders. A company benefits from the stability provided by the states in which it operates. It has a duty to help uphold and not undermine this stability. This means that the company should itself consider broad ethical concerns in considering issues such as remuneration, including the wider impact of high remuneration, and its duty to its shareholders.

There are numerous criticisms of the incentives on executives: many tax structuring schemes incentivise executives both to take risks, and to take early gains at the expense of longer-term results;

markets penalise executives disproportionately for failure to perform in the short term. Equity based incentives and associated deferred payment can encourage longer-term thinking, but there are dangers if the thinking moves too long term: executives become incentivised to stay in post, to accept mediocre performance rather than drive for class-beating. All incentives should work, and all will have unintended consequences. And the corporate world is a competitive one: market conditions will change, the unexpected will happen.

There is no single ethical framework which every company should follow in reaching decisions on how its profits are used and shared. However, any company should have a clear ethical framework to enable it to ensure it has understood when it should be discussing ethical issues and how they should be approached. The purpose of such a framework is to highlight the consequences of the different approaches, to respect the rights of shareholders while also (appropriately) respecting duties to employees and the state. Of course, an ethical framework does not guarantee that a company will behave ethically or be successful – Enron had a 64-page *code of ethics*.

Looking at longstanding and well understood traditions in ethics can provide rules which are applicable, as well as highlighting ethical issues which are difficult to reconcile with major companies but nonetheless can also provide useful insights. Ethical rules have to be prioritised, and the prioritisation has to be transparent, in order to be able to effectively consider the ethical implications of decisions on remuneration, tax and dividends.

Traditional ethics has limitations – first, it is not easy to use ethics to produce hard numbers. Ethical thinking will not provide simple calculations to answer these questions – and attempts to do so will produce damaging unintended consequences. Most abuse is not about numbers, but about the structures and concepts which give rise to high numbers. As suggested by the idea of "render unto Caesar," it is less important to focus on how much has been paid, than whether a payment is merited at all, or whether an unmerited payment is in effect stealing from others. The second failing ethics has is a difficulty in reconciling certain key premises, notably in this case around freedom (of an individual) and equality – the right of each individual to be able to participate fairly in society and in interactions with each other, which is problematic where there are very large differences in wealth.

A structured approach to ethical decisions around sharing profits is both desirable and feasible. It is difficult for a company to resolve well understood conflicts between ethical principles – notably between freedom and some elements of justice. Within the context of an understanding of a company's rights and duties, a company will be unable to prioritise equality, beyond equality of opportunity. This is one of a number of aspects of ethics which a company can support only indirectly, through support for government. It should be noted that government policy can be ambivalent in this area: activities such as lotteries may promote inequality of outcome and inequality of wealth.

Remuneration reports and consideration of ethical issues has improved dramatically since the financial crisis, under the instigation of shareholders as well as regulators and legislators. This process can go further still. What ethics can usefully assist in providing at this stage is a framework of clear prioritised rights and duties, which is missing in many cases. This will help decision making, communication of decisions, and identification of problems. It will never prevent abuse, but its absence or misuse will make abuse more obvious to shareholders.

Investment theory, and corporate finance theory, are highly developed and well understood in the boardroom and by institutional investors. Companies already tend to follow rigorous processes when assessing investment prospects, whether to start a new business, buy shares or expand capacity. The rigour of this process is entirely in keeping with ethical arguments for Justice and Equality (at least equality of opportunity). There is much about modern private sector company management which is in line with established ethical thinking.

A company needs to extend this rigour to be able to specifically consider the broad ethical implications of how it uses its profits:

- for reinvestment or to pay dividends,
- to pay tax,
- to remunerate executives.

As well as considering these issues, it needs to be able to show it has done so, fairly and consistently.

In writing *Ethics in Investment Banking*[4] Ed Newell and I observed that for an organisation to act ethically, it had to inculcate ethics as part of its overall decision making at every level, and there needed to be an opportunity for any employee to question whether an action was ethical.

Cicero argued that the expedient decision is always the honourable decision. Archbishop William Temple said that *"The art of government in fact is the art of so ordering life that self-interest prompts what justice demands."*[5]

There is no single, right and obvious solution to the problems considered here. The key issue is for companies – and their critics – to have a framework to identify and assess ethical issues as an intrinsic part of business decisions, building on duty-based and virtue-based ethical thinking. This requires clear prioritisation of a series of ethical rights and duties:

- *Use of profits*: it is appropriate for a company to consider carefully how to best use its profits, primarily for the benefit of shareholders, but also to accept that a series of other ethical duties exists.
- *Shareholders*: shareholders have a right to earn a return from investment, including to reinvest in the business to create further value or to take out dividends, provided this does not conflict with the company's other ethical duties. A rigorous use of well understood investment appraisal and asset allocation methodologies actively supports the ethical principle of providing equality of opportunity.
- *Employees*: a company should deal fairly with all employees, including directors and executives. Employees at all levels have a duty to respect the rights of shareholders, and not to abuse their positions. Remuneration which is not justified is an unethical transfer of value from shareholder to employee. All unusual remuneration proposals should be subject to individual shareholder votes.
- *Government*: a company has a broad and clear ethical duty to support government. This includes paying appropriate taxes levied by governments. Companies should not be expected to second guess the spirit of legislation, but at the same time should not make use of obvious loopholes. This includes considering cases where changing global commerce has moved so fast as to outdate national and international legislative norms.
- *Customers*: although customers do not receive a share of profits, it must be accepted that a company has a duty of care to customers,

and shareholders via the company should not seek to derive a profit through behaving unethically towards customers.

- *Counterparties*: including customers, supplier and creditors, a company has a range of contractual obligations. Contracts are based on systematically describing a series of promises, which a company has an ethical obligation to honour, before shareholders can take returns.

2
Greed and Self-Interest? Criticism of Corporate Decisions on Sharing Profits

The art of government in fact is the art of so ordering life that self-interest prompts what justice demands.

Archbishop William Temple (1881–1944)
Christianity and Social Order

Chapter summary

- Decisions on how profits are used have ethical implications.
- Companies have been criticised over how executives are remunerated, especially over "payments for failure."
- Multinational companies have been criticised over how tax affairs appear to be managed to minimise taxes paid, in some cases taking account of obvious loopholes.
- Shareholders have sometimes been rather obviously missing from discussions on how companies manage their affairs.
- Criticism of company behaviour is not unbiased. Political criticism is angled at swaying voters, and there is often a gulf between political statement and legislation.
- Examples of extreme abuse in executive remuneration have led to shareholder and popular opposition – including EU caps on bonuses and referendums in Switzerland.
- Key ethical concepts – notably freedom and justice – may be difficult to reconcile with each other.

- The atomisation of specific ethical principles may not be the key to making ethically informed decisions – ethics is the prerogative of an entire company, not just a Board.
- There are a number of highly developed ethical schools of thought which can usefully inform company decision making, stretching far wider than just *business ethics.* Ethics of government can be relevant where decisions affect large numbers of people.
- Non-western philosophical thinking can also be instructive, especially where there is no direct translation of the idea of "ethics," and broader or different approaches are used, such as *Dharma.*

There are significant ethical implications surrounding decisions on the payment of dividends, tax and remuneration, which may affect the long and short-term standing and value of a corporation. As all three are paid from profits, decisions affecting each type of payment are inter-linked, ethically as well as financially.

Companies, notably banks, have been criticised for over-rewarding executives, including paying for "failure." Criticism has been particularly strong in the case of banks making bonus payments when they make losses, or where bonus pools are greater than total dividend payments.

There has been a public excoriation of multinational companies which have aggressively sought to take advantage of legal loopholes to manage their tax affairs, including Amazon and Starbucks. At the same time, the fiduciary duties of directors make it difficult not to seek to – legally – minimise tax payments.

The criticism of "excessive" executive remuneration and "aggressive" tax avoidance appears predominantly to be based on two related concepts: first, that such behaviour undermines the activities of the state; and second, that it undermines equality in society. These criticisms need to be assessed against an understanding of the nature of duty to the state, and the ethical argument for and desirability of equality. The populist portrayal of executive remuneration and of tax avoidance is that these are effectively immoral actions going against the spirit of the law, and tantamount to theft.

In the financial crisis, shareholders were often strangely silent or unrepresented. Shareholders vote (or should vote) to appoint executives and non-executive directors, approve resolutions on a raft of matters including remuneration, and have a significant influence on strategic issues. Shareholders have been criticised for pushing a short-term agenda, with specific concerns over the dangers of over-reaction to quarterly financial reporting, and for encouraging higher risks in the pursuit of higher *returns*. Trustees, who are responsible for selecting investment managers, remain at a remove from the companies in which the funds they invest have shareholdings. The position of trustees is complex: generally not financial professionals, but with huge moral and legal responsibility. The training of trustees has rightly become a more high profile issue. Trustees may in some cases rely too heavily on specialist consultants, who may be risk averse in their advice, in particular avoiding innovation.

Boards of major companies, making contentious decisions are generally not "deaf or blind" to public criticism (as the former Chairman of a major bank described it), but faced with a range of choices, none of which in practice are palatable.

The complexities and context of criticism

The context of such criticisms isn't always straightforward (it can be rather complex), and it is important that this context is understood.

Political criticism of companies is certainly not automatically free from bias and needs to be understood in context. Whereas some of the criticism may be valid, equally some criticism of the behaviour of companies may be incorrect, and some may be made for electoral purposes. For example, attempts early in the financial crisis to blame the decline in shares and currencies on *speculation* by *hedge funds* now seems clearly misplaced, but may have served a political purpose in defusing criticism against governments. Government does not feel constrained to follow the ethics which constrain individuals, for a combination of reasons: first, because individuals support government and form governments to provide a type of protection and support which it is not possible for individuals to carry out without some form of society in place. Consequently, it can be appropriate for government to take action – using arms, or incarcerating citizens for example – which would not be appropriate for an individual to do, but which is supported by individual citizens. Second, government may as a matter of expediency (reluctantly) break rules, or give itself separate laws, accepting that its behaviour is justified by the ends it achieves although the means are questionable (what Kierkegaard described as the "teleological suspension of the ethical"), or because the consequences of not breaking some rules would give rise to an unjust or unethical result (i.e., allowing a violent riot rather than using force to break it up). Third, government may abuse its powers and act unethically – because it passes laws and can get away with it. Separating these different drivers of behaviours can sometimes be contentious.

The issue of excessive executive pay has led to shareholder revolts at major quoted companies, notably among banks such as Barclays, and has led to two referenda seeking to cap executive remuneration in Switzerland, where Novartis proposed a €75 million retirement package for its departing Chairman (one was successful, one unsuccessful – see below).

Shareholders have suffered significant losses in the financial crisis, but shareholder demands for higher returns increased the risk taken by banks and was one of the causes of the crisis. Trustees of investment funds have been largely silent about their part in the investment cycle, despite the pressure some trustees place on fund managers for short-term/quarterly returns.

Up to a point Lord Copper

To what extent is the criticism of companies justified? Much of the political and media criticism of companies tends to focus only on tax and remuneration, and does not focus on returns to shareholders. Any balanced analysis of behaviour regarding tax and remuneration must also include consideration of shareholders. Equally, to understand behaviour of companies, the incentives put in place by government on behalf of the wider population must be considered, and business ethics cannot be viewed outside of the context of societal ethics more generally.

As a starting point, corporations need to make substantive decisions on how to share profits between shareholders, employees and the state. Over time, there is significant scope for discretion in how these various stakeholders are treated, and decisions regarding one group inevitably have significant implications for the other two groups.

Applying ethical principles to financial decisions is not always straightforward, but nonetheless specific and informed ethical thinking is necessary to prevent abuses, the over-rewarding of one group at the expense of the others, and to ensure that decisions take long-term issues affecting value into account. Abusive decisions can have long-term, rather than or in addition to short-term, consequences. This can come from changing the risk of a business, and transferring risk from, for example, the shareholder to customers or the state.

Business ethics must draw from mainstream ethical thinking, including political ethics, in order to inform directors of major companies on how to approach the decisions they make and the challenges they face – in many ways, the type of decision faced by the Board of an international company is more similar to concepts of political decision making than the traditional suppositions of personal ethics (hence this book's examination of Cicero and other political philosophers).

The political and public focus on business behaviour, notably on the notion of the payment of tax as being an intrinsic duty of a company, shows the conflation of business and political ethics, and the way that business ethics cannot be separated from other areas of activity. Companies can be constrained or even punished by an act of political will for ethical breaches which do not breach the law. For example, the UK's proposed cap on excessive or usurious interest rates for payday lenders has curtailed their profitability, even though they broke no laws. At least arguably, the lack of legislation placing a cap on the cost of loans is an example of government failure – with poor financial education resulting in a large group of people who cannot understand the costs of financing, there is an ethical obligation on government to intervene in this market.

Business ethics reflects the ethics of society in general. We should not be surprised to see everyday failings reflected in the boardroom – company directors are not appointed because of their saintliness. Political and media commentary can exacerbate a perception of a difference in standards which may not be borne out by close scrutiny.

Debate between ethical principles of justice (Rawls) and freedom (Kant) is not capable of a simple resolution. However, the key issue isn't so much to be able to determine a definitive approach to ethics, as to be able to articulate an ethical stance and know how to consider issues with an ethical dimension. This can be demonstrated by looking at potential alternative frameworks. Perhaps, rather surprisingly, a business could end up adopting the approach of Cicero in *De Oficiis*, more commonly seen as of relevance to the political sphere. This may resonate because modern corporate decision making affects numerous bodies of people, in the way that politics has complex effects.

Timothy Geithner, who was previously President of the Federal Reserve Bank of New York, was appointed US Treasury Secretary in 2009, remaining in this post until 2013. Not having an investment banking background may have assisted him in looking relatively neutrally at the financial crisis, although he has been criticised for supposedly having been "captured" by the banking industry.

In an interview with Andrew Ross Sorkin of the *New York Times* titled "What Timothy Geithner Really Thinks,"[1] Geithner defended his approach to the Toxic Asset Restructuring Programme (TARP) in the US, and compared it with the approach in the UK. TARP was used to support banks facing severe problems in relation to capital and funding for their operations. In the UK, the government took populist methods to accompany the *restructuring* of banks (notably RBS and Lloyds), including restrictions on bonuses, and a requirement on banks to lend to small businesses – one major impact of the financial crisis was a reduction in credit available, especially to small companies whose credit quality was impaired, or was difficult to assess.

Geithner's commentary on the attempts in the UK to manage popular opinion by capping bonuses and putting requirements on banks to lend are dismissive: "those are largely fake, and they were sort of ridiculous, because their economy was way overleveraged, too, and lending was going to fall even in the best sort of circumstances. And did it help the British in terms of taking some of the sting out of the public anger? No...It wasn't really designed to change comp. It was designed to create the impression that they were changing comp. Did it significantly diminish the popular version of what they did and make them more popular for doing it? No. Was it effective? No."

Commenting specifically on the competence and level of ethics in the investment banking sector, Geithner writes "My jobs mostly exposed me to talented senior bankers, and selection bias probably gave me an impression that the U.S. financial sector was more capable and ethical than it really was."[2]

It is also interesting to note that *HMRC* appears to have tightened up its approach to collecting corporate taxes during the financial crisis, presumably as a way of improving the UK's sovereign financial position and securing the UK's *credit rating*, which may in a number of cases have had the opposite effect of the drive to lend more to small businesses.

According to Geithner, when he asked former US President Bill Clinton how he could satisfy popular opinion Mr Clinton said,

> *[I] could take Lloyd Blankfein into a dark alley. And slit his throat, and it would satisfy them for about two days. Then the blood lust would rise again.*[3]

In the light of clear differences between:

- political statements and policy;
- the publicly stated onus on companies and the actions of governments,

it seems unreasonable, and potentially damaging, for companies to aim to satisfy the spirit of the law when it comes to tax payment, when that spirit is generally rather cloudy (more absinthe than vodka).

For the Board of a bank in receipt of public funds, the question of priorities becomes very stark: to maximise the recovery by government of its funds, the Board may need to retain areas of business which require spending a certain level on salaries, which is publicly and therefore politically unpopular. To fail to retain these business lines may prejudice the return of government funding, thereby damaging public finances. To pay the salaries required may not be politically possible. As with other cases of remuneration, this properly becomes a question for shareholders. The answer from government in the case of Lloyds and RBS appears to be that if the bank is clearly making rapid progress, then it is reasonable to pay relatively high salaries. The answer in the other cases – where a bank does not appear to make sufficient progress, is that paying salaries cannot be justified, even though this may be for short-term electoral purposes. In the US, tight limits were put in place for payments for executives at banks in receipt of federal funds to bail them out, with the US Pay Czar setting a clear maximum base salary of $500,000 for 75 out of the top 100 employees of four major companies in receipt of bail-out money including Citigroup, General Motors, AIG and GMAC.

Longstanding ethical traditions have an important part to play

The analysis of the ethics of behaviour and decisions has been around for at least 3,000 years. The level of thinking, questioning, analysis and refinement has been very substantial. Business ethics as a separate discipline started to evolve seriously only within the last 50 years, and does not reflect either the full extent of ethical tradition, or the rapid pace of change in business. Just as economists may need to wait for data to emerge to analyse what has driven business decisions, so with philosophers and ethicists.

Much of ethical thinking – but by no means all of it – stems from religious traditions. This thinking is often relevant to businesses, and can be very refined in applying ethics to practical issues. Traditions relevant to political decision making and government are also relevant to company decision making, especially where companies are making decisions affecting large numbers of people.

Maybe ethics isn't the answer? Lessons from other philosophical traditions

Philosophical traditions in India, Japan and China can also be instructive. In many cases, there is no direct translation of "ethics." The Buddhist concept of *Dharma* is sometimes used as a translation of ethics, but is actually broader (at least than a precise or academic use of ethics) and by definition is an aspect of everything in life, and cannot be confined to individual aspects of activity. This, and similar concepts in Indian and Japanese traditions can therefore be useful in reconciling apparently irreconcilable differences in ethical approaches.

If the explanation of, and principles behind, business ethics are radically different from normal societal or personal ethics, then there is something wrong. Just as it is wrong for an individual to kill a neighbour, equally it is wrong for a business to do so, or to tolerate a situation where its employees are killed. Some groups are concerned about the impact of extractive industries on the environment, especially those involved in hydro-carbon (oil, gas, coal etc.) production. However, it is questionable how we can see extraction of minerals as unethical *per se* in a situation where as an individual is concerned it is not considered to be unethical to use for example an electric light ultimately fuelled by a coal or gas fired power station, or to use a car which uses hydrocarbons as fuel. What may at first look like reasonable principles, may on examination prove to be flawed, and a considered ethical framework will reduce the risk of (i) *moral relativism* resulting in lax ethical standards, and (ii) draconian and ultimately unworkable or excessively punitive ethical rules.

Business ethics must act as a synthesis of ethical principles which would be applied to an individual and (especially in the case of large companies) which would be applied to a government. It is acceptable for a government to have regard specifically to its own citizens, rather than all people globally. Equally, it is acceptable for a company to have regard to its own activities, and not to see correcting social ills as a priority part of its activities.

A large company may well be significantly more global in outlook than an individual government. Globalisation is now a recurring theme in investigating ethical issues surrounding the management of companies and around investment. In ethical as well as government terms, we are at the early stages of understanding the impact of globalisation and how to deal with it. Global companies need to be cognizant of ethical challenges as much as operational ones, at the minimum in order to protect value for their shareholders, and maybe in order to retain customers in the long term. Investors struggle to manage the process of applying ethical standards outside their home markets, but also to avoid what might be termed neo-imperialism, requiring companies from very different cultural backgrounds to apply one specific set of cultural standards of behaviour.

The atomisation of "ethics" into finite codes or sets of legalistic principles is bound to fail, and misses the point as far as most philosophical ethical traditions are concerned. "Business ethics" should not be confused with the narrow and disciplinary-related context of professional ethics within a single profession – the ethics applicable to lawyers or doctors, for example, reflect a necessarily narrow approach to professional responsibilities, which is insufficiently broad to apply in many cases to the range of decisions and effects of a major company.

As we will come on to, ethical thinking in particular around equality may actually be consistent with much financially based decision making on new investment.

3
Examining the Issues

Who steals my purse steals trash; 'tis something, nothing;
'twas mine, 'tis his, and has been slave to thousands;
But he that filches from me my good name
Robs me of that which not enriches him,
And makes me poor indeed.

William Shakespeare, *Othello*

Chapter summary

- Banking remuneration is widely seen as a major contribution to the financial crisis, which has had a widespread and very damaging impact on people who had no direct benefit from the previous success of the banking sector.
- Bonus arrangements in *investment banking* – especially for banks bailed out by the taxpayer – look out of balance with the rest of society, especially frozen public sector pay.
- Tax structuring by international companies, both in the old and new economies, can take advantage of loopholes in legislation, which has struggled to adapt to the rapid pace of change in global trade, especially with regard to international co-operation.
- *Advisers* on tax and wealth managers have been criticised and fined for assisting in tax evasion, bringing together the ethics of business and the ethics of wealthy individuals.
- There have been high profile company abuses across a range of other issues – including journalistic standards and phone hacking,

human rights, health and safety – indicating widespread low standards and poor understanding of and interest in ethics.

- The short-term focus of investors in quoted companies has been cited as the cause for poor decision making by Boards. However, institutional investors may hold shares in a given company for longer than the tenure of the average CEO, and short-termism may not be an adequate explanation for behaviour.
- Incentives on decision makers give rise to an asynchronous risk, but blaming short-termism for the wide variety of ethical short-comings is a simplistic explanation for a complex problem.

Business in general, and in particular large companies, have complex ethical issues to consider in relation to how their profits are shared between shareholders, the state and employees.

In general, for the purposes of this book, it is assumed that executives generally make reasonable decisions about the use of profits and cash flow to reinvest in the business, in the form of capital assets (as well as in attracting customers, through marketing, discounting etc.).

There are a number of specific issues it is possible to consider relating to how companies treat employees and the state. It is important to examine these underlying issues, and the political and media discussion relating to them, in some detail to establish an informed frame of reference in order to assess their ethical implications.

Two issues it is possible to look at in some detail are the remuneration of bank Board members and senior executives, and the tax structuring carried out by multinational companies.

There are additional areas which give rise to concern over corporate behaviour which also relate to the standard of ethics in business, which are also worth examining. (The examples given here are not all especially egregious, but have been chosen because they are high profile and many readers will recognise them and already be aware of the background issues.)

Remuneration as a contributor to the banking collapse/ financial crisis

There is a question over whether either or both of the structure of incentives or the level of remuneration might undermine a company. For example, does the payment of multi-million packages to senior executives create a culture of arrogance, or does the risk created by highly incentivised packages with little downside risk lead to investment bankers making reckless decisions?

This book takes the term "remuneration" as being generally relevant and accurate in describing how employees are rewarded and/or paid for their services to an employer. Remuneration can be described in differing ways: earnings, salary, remuneration, *compensation* and so on. The term "remuneration" can be taken as including benefits (pensions, healthcare costs, bonuses, commissions etc.). Sometimes this is described as "total remuneration." Investment banks typically describe remuneration as "compensation," presumably in recognition of the sacrifices that bankers are expected to make to perform their jobs.

Former UK Prime Minister Gordon Brown compared the funding gap of UK banks with the level of remuneration paid, describing "excessive remuneration at the expense of adequate capitalisation" in his book *Beyond the Crash*.

It seems clear from the very large sums lost by the leaders of failed investment banks during the financial crisis that there was a problem of understanding of the risks involved, and not just a problem of imprudent risk-taking. In addition, the wealth in these cases was typically in the form of equity (or shares) in the bank itself, reducing the differential in interests between employees and shareholders. The CEOs of Lehman and Bear Stearns, two investment banks which failed during the crisis, individually lost huge sums of money (many hundreds of millions). Part of the proposed solution to financial instability includes remuneration in equity rather than cash. Ownership of very large sums of equity did not prevent failures in the past.

There is an incentive for executives and senior employees to take high risks: the upside relates to the remuneration resulting from the profits earned, the downside relates to loss of a job and a salary, but rarely a capital loss. The incentives are such that they are greater for employees who have not yet built up significant equity holdings (or who have hedged their exposure to a possible fall in the share price of their employer). At a young age, the idea of an "Acapulco Trade" can be compelling, and the real risks difficult to understand. An Acapulco Trade is a term used to describe a very high-risk, possibly not fully authorised large trade, which would be very profitable if successful, and highly damaging if not. The concept is that a trader would place the trade, then leave for Acapulco, only returning if the trade is successful. It is unclear to what extent this concept is apocryphal, as in reality many large trades do not result in an immediate or overnight conclusion.

The greed of banking executives may have played no more a part in the failure of banks in practice than a combination of: poor management training, poor adherence to existing rules, weak *regulation* and fast changing global markets.

The breadth (or lack of it) of training for candidates for senior management roles may also be a key factor. Banks tend to promote the most successful bankers at specific areas of activity, and then progressively give them more responsibility. In many cases, this is not accompanied by much formal training in management. Many banks are managed in a fairly feudal manner, with individual bankers dependant on the patronage and support of a senior banker, who expects a clear demonstration of personal (as opposed to institutional) loyalty from subordinates. In some countries, notably the US but also some Asian markets, the MBA has become a commonplace qualification for senior executives in investment banking, although this appears less current in Europe. Most MBA courses now offer, or make compulsory, the study of ethics. However, this is a relatively recent development (and it will be interesting to see how long ethics remains compulsory).

The culture of turning a blind eye to employees – paying lip-service to internal rules, while in practice encouraging behaviour which breaches rules but is believed to be in the company's interests – is probably as much a cause of the financial crisis as the level of incentives themselves, although it is probably impossible to prove this one way or the other.

The pace of change in financial products, and the size of increasingly global markets, clearly took banks and regulators by surprise. Banking CEOs should have had, in a number of cases, a better understanding of the risks they were allowing. At the same time, it is clear from other perspectives that the impact of connected and inter-connected markets and financial products is still causing surprises to governments and regulators. Much of the financial crisis was not novel, but was presaged by similar problems in previous crises:

- *Sovereign debt* crises are nothing new, and have been seen in Latin America in the 1980s and early 1990s, in Russia after 1997, and in the UK in the late 1970s.

- The proximate cause of the credit crisis was the *mis-selling* of mort-gages in the US. There have been widespread problems of mis-selling of financial products – insurance in many markets and the flagrant mis-selling of dotcom securities.

It is difficult to simply say that bank executives "should" have under-stood and are culpable for not having done so, when it is clear that regulators and governments in some ways have still not been able to grip the complexities of global financial markets, and there are repeated instances of known problems which have still not been remedied.

There appear to be a number of reasonable conclusions relating to the incentivisation within investment banks:

- Incentives affect behaviour. Incentives which encourage risky behaviour create risk in an organisation. This has to be dealt with by properly constructed and observed management systems.
- The remuneration structures and levels in banking contributed to the financial crisis, but were not solely responsible. The incen-tives and commissions paid to mortgage sale agents may have had a bigger impact.
- The internationalisation of financial markets and the increased inter-connectedness of markets and institutions fundamentally changes risk, and this change has not been properly reflected in changes to the way companies and markets are regulated or managed.

Assisting in tax evasion

On 21 May 2014, US Attorney General Eric Holder announced that one of the world's largest banks, Credit Suisse AG, had pleaded guilty to charges of a conspiracy to assist clients over decades in evading taxes through the use of undisclosed bank accounts. Credit Suisse agreed to pay $1.8 billion in fines ($1.13 billion) and restitution ($670 million) to the IRS, the US tax authorities.

This case came in the aftermath of the financial crisis, at a time when there was still overriding concern about the capitalisation of major banks. Offsetting this is the very significant political focus both on raising taxes, and on being seen to collect taxes due from the "1 per cent."

Investment bank bonus pools

A large group of shareholders of UK banking group Barclays have reacted very negatively to the proposals for a bonus pool in 2014 (of £2.38 billion), when the total proposed bonus pool is a multiple of the proposed (unchanged) dividend payment. A total of 34 per cent of shareholders who voted did not back the remuneration report at the company's AGM on 24 April 2014. Alison Kennedy, governance and stewardship director at Standard Life, said: "We are unconvinced that the amount of the 2013 bonus pool was in the best interests of shareholders, particularly when we consider how the bank's profits are divided amongst employees, shareholders and ongoing investment in the business. The dividend was unchanged in the year and an additional £5.8 billion of capital was raised from shareholders. We also believe that this decision has had negative repercussions on the bank's reputation".[1]

The company, in taking the view that it is necessary to invest in retaining staff in order to preserve value, has highlighted the tension between employees and shareholders which can exist. In this case, the bonus arrangements go very significantly wider than Board members. The Chair of the Barclays Remuneration Committee, Sir John Sunderland, replied (very clearly) to the criticism: "Compensation in the financial services industry is far too high but we cannot take the risk of acting unilaterally. Do you imagine we want to pay anyone in the bank more than we have to? Do you imagine I and the chairman seek the level of invective that has been poured upon us?".[2]

Barclays is not at all alone in this decision: RBS has not paid dividends since it benefited from a government bail-out, and has continued to pay some bonuses (albeit at a relatively low level).

The consideration of bonus levels within investment banks can be straightforward in a good operating environment. A bonus pool will be designated based on a percentage of revenue (or profits), which takes account of shareholder *returns* (via dividends), other costs, taxes and so on. Management of the investment bank will then allocate this around individual business units, and in turn their management will allocate the pool among individual employees.

In a year when business performance is such that there is no significant scope for a bonus pool, then the investment bank's shareholders will have to decide whether to pay above normal thresholds. This can be seen as both shareholders subsidising employees, and shareholders making an investment in the business.

The situation is typified by the following consideration:

- A number of business units within the investment bank will have been highly profitable, even if the overall investment bank's profits were not sufficient to sustain the anticipated bonus pool.
- A small number of key individuals will be very mobile – meaning they are both able to move to another highly paid role elsewhere (pretty much immediately) and have the inclination to do so if their employer, in their eyes, does not honour their obligations to pay the individual for that individual's performance.
- An investment bank has two types of capital: financial and human. Separating out which type is the source of revenue and profits is not always straightforward. However, drawing a distinction between high and low performing individuals is at least theoretically possible, and this can be used to benchmark the value to an organisation of individuals.
- Some individuals will have contracts which specify minimum bonus levels (although this is less common than previously), and others may have agreements which specify formulae for bonus payments.
- Investment banks have evolved a "high bonus-low basic" structure historically, in order to minimise risk and also avoid paying underperforming employees.
- The impact of the bonus culture within investment banks, together with typically relatively selfish line management, has been to encourage individual investment bankers to continuously monitor external job opportunities – investment bankers are not always encouraged to stay comfortably in a role, and the annual cycle of appraising bonuses and performance means that frequently historic dedication and success can be irrelevant within a single year.
- A difference needs to be clearly drawn between executive remuneration and investment banking bonus pools, in that executives (i.e., executive Board members) typically receive a much higher level of fixed remuneration than investment bankers, and therefore the circumstances under which bonuses can be merited are different

than those for investment bankers, who may be paid significantly lower fixed salaries than in other equivalent professions.

The Board and remuneration committee of a company in Barclays' situation is seeking to act in shareholders' interests by maximising the value for the shareholder overall, taking a view that a deterioration in the investment bank is likely to outweigh the value from reinvesting by subsidising bonuses at the expense of dividends. Shareholders ultimately earn a total shareholder return (TSR) from dividends plus the appreciation in the capital value of a share.

Determining the level of a bonus pool is more complicated when, in the light of public shareholder dissatisfaction, many capable investment bankers will look to see if there are other more stable opportunities elsewhere. Consequently, a Board which proposes remuneration resulting in shareholder rebellion is less likely to be able to preserve value for shareholders through subsidising a bonus pool. The Board is acting for shareholders, and in the end needs to act with shareholder consent. Uncertainty around shareholders' long-term support for a strategy or for investment is destabilising for employees and therefore for clients (and probably not the other way round – that is, clients won't be destabilised before employees, given that investment banking clients have a demonstrated capacity for following individual investment bankers as well as institutions). Strategically, this situation shows the difficulty in particular market circumstances of a commercial banking and a full-service investment bank operating under single ownership. However, in circumstances where there is greater profit from both banking and investment banking, then there is significant synergy between the two – effectively the ability to cycle capital from low-return commercial banking to high-return investment banking, and the provision of high-margin services through an investment bank to a commercial banking client-base.

The position at Barclays does not explicitly set out how individual investment bankers with different levels of performance will be paid, but rather provides details of a total bonus pool. It is likely that Barclays will seek to pay high performers in line with their market rate, and will seek to pay poor performers little or no bonus.

Recent cases of corporate tax structuring – Google/Starbucks

·Criticism of Google and Starbucks has been particularly striking because of the profile of the two companies: two very successful businesses with global presence, one built on the new economy, one engaged in the centuries-old business of coffee houses.

In the UK, Google was criticised extensively for paying a very low rate of tax – £3.4 million on revenue of £3.2 billion. Google transactions were "closed" in Ireland, removing them from UK taxation. An exchange at the end of the evidence given by Matt Brittin of Google to the Commons Public Account Committee on 16 May 2013 summarises the criticism and defence of "aggressive" tax structuring. Margaret Hodge, the Chair of the Committee, described: "unethical behaviour in deliberately manipulating the reality of your business to avoid paying your fair share of tax to the common good" and asked "How do you think ordinary people feel?"

In reply, Matt Brittin of Google said "I think if ordinary people listened to that statement, they would rightly be concerned, but that statement is not a fair representation of how we operate. We comply fully with the laws that are set down by politicians and we operate in the UK in a way that is consistent with other companies operating from a European headquarters outside the UK."[3]

The first part of this bases behaviour on doing what is legal: this is an established explanation for all kinds of behaviour, in both business and personal life. The second part of this reply can be assessed as based on a form of "moral relativism" – it is asserting that behaviour is acceptable because it is common. The legalistic answer is not sufficient from an ethical perspective, but neither is it necessarily an indication that the action is incorrect. The second answer is essentially *utilitarian*, but in many ethical traditions it would be viewed as relatively meaningless, because it can be used to justify almost any action.

In the same committee, Lin Homer, Chief Executive of *HMRC* highlighted a gap between the tax that is collected and expectations of how tax should be collected from companies, saying: "What we cannot do, unless and until you change the law, is collect the tax that people would like us to collect."

Ms Homer's statement is presumably carefully considered, and is interesting from the perspective that it is entirely understandable that (i) HMRC will understand the limitations of their powers, and (ii) HMRC will seek to collect as much tax as possible, in particular to avoid political criticism (after all, the Chief Executive of HMRC is a political appointment). It is therefore reasonable to assume that her statement is made advisedly, and is technically correct.

In an article in the *Observer* (18 May 2013) Eric Schmidt, Executive Chairman of Google, defended his company's approach to taxation, indicating that he was following established laws "most developed countries, including the UK, have worked together to create a set of tax treaties." This, he said, obeyed rules laid out by politicians and that Google paid appropriate levels of tax in the US. "We pay more taxes in the US than in any other country – around $2 billion in corporate income taxes to the US government in 2012. It's the same for UK-based technology or pharmaceutical companies, which pay the majority of their corporation tax in the UK, as that is where most of the activity that generates their profits takes place."

Starbucks, a US-based owner of coffee shops, has been one of a number of businesses singled out for criticism as well as Google. Whereas some of the criticism of Google can be considered in the light of the difficulty of developing tax statutes for the internet, Starbuck's business model does not centre around the internet, but the high street. Starbuck's corporate structure involves a European head office in the Netherlands, which receives (brand-related) royalties, and a coffee procurement business centred in Switzerland, and which applies a margin when selling coffee to Starbucks in the UK.

It has been accepted for some considerable time that large corporations would manage their tax affairs actively. There has been a spectrum of different approaches to paying tax, structuring financing and legal entities. This has been more or less transparent. In practice, the Head of Tax at most major companies would be able to agree to a tax settlement for a tax year with their tax authorities, which was based on an overall understanding of a tax position, and not just a line by line calculation.

However, there have been a number of factors which have crystallised a changed approach by many governments to aggressive tax optimisation, notably the development of internet based shopping has led to many retailers having no substantial physical presence, giving them the ability to make choices on the location of their activities on a different basis than was previously feasible. Also, the reduction in tax receipts during the financial crisis has led to finance ministries seeking to reduce tax avoidance generally in the economy, in order to improve their financial position.

The tax affairs of Google and Starbucks, and their relatively unconvincing defence of their behaviour in front of government committees, raise the question of how far it is reasonable to go in pursuing tax efficiency. The position of Google looks difficult to defend, and appears to be managed to maximise tax efficiency. Probably the main bank involved in the tax structuring "industry," Barclays, has now closed down its tax structuring activities. The profitability of this activity was never actively reported, but it is likely to have been responsible for a meaningful proportion of the profits of Barclays Capital, the investment banking arm of Barclays. This reflects both a change in attitude by Barclays regarding its business model, but also a hardening stance by the UK and other governments relating to the more aggressive approaches to tax structuring.

The OECD

The problems facing governments arising from the change in trade to become more international are recognised and the subject of concern. The OECD – a club for major economies – has developed a detailed program looking into the issue, the OECD Base Erosion and Profit Shifting Project. The OECD states that companies moving activities to areas with low or no tax "undermines the fairness and integrity of tax systems."[4] The OECD Council, in its "Declaration on Base Erosion and Profit Shifting"[5] itemises a number of areas for collaborative action by the OECD and the G20 group of countries. These include issues relating to globalisation and the digital economy, tax avoidance and also measures relating to "intangibles."

The OECD's members include countries which have used taxation as a means to attract investment, (Switzerland, Ireland), and countries with flat taxes (Russia) as well as countries with progressive tax systems (the UK), countries which assert worldwide taxation (the United States) and countries which do not, (such as Hong Kong). It is interesting that these very variable tax regimes see threats from the same sources, notably "double non-taxation" arising from exploiting asymmetries in domestic and international tax rules. At the same time, the scale of difference suggests that the governments concerned do not share the same view of the detailed concepts of the ethics of taxation.

Ethical concerns in business – Is there a connecting theme?

In trying to understand the financial crisis, it is relatively straightforward to look at thematic flaws in ethical standards relating to two major issues: first, mis-selling (which also affects many other areas of business and society) and second, conflicts of interest. Looking at a wider range of industries, ethical concerns cover a wide spectrum of behaviour. The examples given here, taken from a range of sectors, relate to remuneration, tax structuring, human rights, safety, the environment and media. There is not a simple discernible pattern to the behaviour, and as set out in Chapter 4, this reflects ethical issues in society more widely.

Reaching an understanding of the basis for the ethical concerns raised in the areas looked at here, and the behaviour under scrutiny, must be based on the decision-making process, and the inculcation of ethical thinking into the decision-making process, in a company.

To what extent is it possible to separate what is a legitimate desire to maximise shareholder value, from unethical behaviour which can lead to an actual reduction in long-term value?

Looking further at other areas of concern regarding business ethics can help assess whether any clear position can be taken.

High Frequency Trading

Michael Lewis has shone a light into High Frequency Trading (HFT) in his 2014 book *Flash Boys*. This raises the question as to how far it is fair to go to prosper from an advantage over others in the same market, making a challenging comparison and assessing whether HFT is ethically similar to *insider dealing*, or it is an area of legitimate business advantage.

There is a crucial difference between HFT and insider dealing. This lies in the inevitability that insider dealing is based on an abuse of privileged information (even if at second hand). The conclusion in "Ethics in Investment Banking" was that insider dealing was unethical specifically on that basis.

Is HFT in reality no more than developing a more efficient infrastructure to trade more effectively – essentially no different from a fishing vessel which sails faster back to harbour to be the first to sell a catch? The potential unfairness of HFT in this situation is that other market participants may not have understood what was happening. However, that is not a unique instance (in fact, finding markets which provide precise equality of information is rather difficult).

Alternatively, could HFT be ethically more complex than the fishing analogy, as the traders concerned are profiting from other traders, rather than primarily from their own activity? This is probably more accurate, but at the same time it is based on HFT using ingenuity and sometimes significant investment in order to gain an advantage. Perhaps this is more similar to many market traders than fishermen in that the HFT traders do not themselves land the fish. To consider this to be per se unethical is potentially to consider a lot of *derivative* activity unethical – including discount retailing for example.

It is difficult to conclude that HFT is in itself actually unethical. It may reinforce the importance of exchanges ensuring they are transparent in explaining how they work, and how traders are using them. To the extent, of course, that they themselves understand.

Phone hacking

The attention paid to the phone hacking scandal in the UK has resulted in a review by a senior judge (Lord Leveson), the closure of the UK's most popular tabloid newspaper, the *Sun*, and the trial on criminal charges of newspaper editors and even the press advisor to the UK's Prime Minister.

Journalists, notably at newspapers owned by News International, had frequently hacked the mobile phone accounts of high profile people, including the voice messages of a murdered child. This practice had continued for a considerable period of time.

It can be asked whether the organisations in question were at some level prepared to suspend ethical standards in order to achieve business success. It is unclear to what extent this related to achieving corporate targets, or alternatively lax professional standards by journalists.

The governance of News Corporation, the controlling shareholder of News International, was brought into question as a result of concerns over phone hacking and the management of News International's newspapers. Following a failure to receive assurances from News Corporation, the Church of England's Ethical Investment Advisory Group recommended disinvestment from News Corporation due to concerns over its standards of corporate governance.

ABACUS-AC1

The high profile investigation of Goldman Sachs over the structuring and marketing of a mortgage backed security highlighted key issues in the ethics of investment banking. The appearance of Goldman Sachs executives in front of a US Senate committee highlighted both the expectations of politicians regarding business behaviour, and the approach of some businesses:

> *A Wall Street culture that, while it may once have been focused on serving clients and promoting commerce, is now all too simply self-serving. The ultimate harm is not just to clients poorly served by their investment banks. It's to all of us.* (Senator Carl Levin, 27 April 2010, statement to the Senate Permanent Subcommittee on Investigations)

> *[T]he nature of the principal business in market making is that we are the other side of what our clients want to do.* (Lloyd Blankfein, CEO of the Goldman Sachs Group Inc., 27 April 2010, testimony to the Senate Permanent Subcommittee on Investigations)

ABACUS was a structured security, with value related to investments in an underlying basket of mortgage-related securities. The issuer of the security, Goldman Sachs, had created this basket based on instruments which in its own view were poor value, and one *hedge fund* client had taken a short position (sold securities which it did not own) in the same securities, standing to profit significantly if the value of ABACUS would fall (which it did).

Goldman settled a civil fraud suit brought by the *Securities and Exchange Commission* (*SEC*) without admitting liability. Senator Levin told Mr Blankfein starkly "And you want people to trust you, I would not trust you." The position of a market leading company developing and selling products to its customers (Goldman argued that these were not "clients" in a fiduciary sense) raises fundamental questions, including how clients choose service providers. Businesses are most interested in selecting service providers which can effectively serve them, rather than relying on a service provider's ethical reputation or standards.

Deepwater Horizon – Macondo

On 20 April 2010 there was an explosion and fire on the Deepwater Horizon rig at the Macondo prospect in the Gulf of Mexico. The rig was owned by Transocean, and being operated on behalf of BP.

A series of failures led to a major oil spill with substantial resulting damage, and the death of 11 people.

In the case of BP, there were a number of factors which augmented ethical concerns over an obviously already extreme situation. These included the company's previous experience of fatal accidents in North America, including a fire at the Texas City refinery on 23 March 2005, where 15 people died. The BP senior management's reaction to the criticism levelled at the company inflamed opinion as it appeared to understate the seriousness of the situation. The then CEO's comment "I'd like my life back" following the Deepwater Horizon accident appeared to underscore a perception of a cavalier response to the disaster. At the AGM following the accident, BP even reappointed the same non-executive director as Chair of its Health and Safety Committee (which was surprisingly supported by the vast majority of BP's shareholders).

Killing and seriously injuring employees, customers and contractors would clearly be an egregious breach of ethical standards. There are some industries where the nature of activities results in a significantly heightened risk of major accidents, notably extractive industries (mining, oil exploration and production). There are other areas of activity where risk of injury and death are accepted, for example armed forces and rescue services. In all these cases, negligence and a corporate culture tolerant of negligence would be major ethical failings.

Fossil fuels

There have been calls and campaigns for institutional investors to disinvest from companies whose activities centre on the production of fossil fuels. These calls are based on concern over environmental damage caused by fossil fuel use (rather than extraction), and the damage that this causes especially in developing countries.

A group called Operation Noah has been involved with a campaign called "Bright Now," calling for Church investors to take action including disinvest from fossil fuels. The action they seek includes:

- disinvest from companies involved in the extraction of fossil fuels;
- take a leading and influential role in the national debate on the ethics of investment in fossil fuels;
- support the development of clean alternatives to fossil fuels through their investment policies.

There are complex problems with this approach to fossil fuels:

* It does not provide an alternative: there is no reliable large-scale alternative energy source available to replace fossil fuels. If the logical conclusion of the disinvestment campaign were reached, and further fossil fuels were not used, the results would be catastrophic in human terms (maybe not so in ecological terms, although this may also be unclear). Although there are alternatives to energy production, they are not sufficient or economical enough to be a widespread solution to replacing hydrocarbons at the current time.
* There is no equivalent condemnation of the demand-side of the activity – that is, individuals using hydrocarbon fuels in their homes and cars, nor is there a clear statement over how users of fossil fuels should act: that is, if it is unethical for a Church to invest in an oil-producing company, should members of the same Church continue to buy fuel from Shell, Exxon, BP or others? In a possibly equivalent situation, the criminalisation of drugs targets both producers and users of illegal substances.
* It can look (and be) oppressive to people in developing countries. In many countries, it is argued that the developed West/North has benefited from extraction of easily accessed and used fossil fuels, which has given rising incomes and a high level of industrial development. Therefore plans to prevent further global access to fossil fuels will enshrine high levels of inequality, in favour of the existing developed economies. The approach could therefore be considered a form of neo-colonial oppression.

It is difficult to conclude therefore that, on balance, the ethical basis for proposing disinvestment in fossil fuel producers and users is justified.

Vedanta

Quoted mining company Vedanta Resources plc has been subject to criticism over the impact of its activities at sites in India on environmental and human rights issues in local communities surrounding its alumina refinery in Lanjigarh, Orissa, and planned bauxite mine in the nearby Niyamgiri hills. The Norwegian Pension fund and others disinvested in 2008–09 from Vedanta as a result of concerns over its activities. There has been a complex pattern of litigation by and against the company in Orissa and in Indian courts.

There are residual concerns over the extent to which concerns from European investors can be appropriately applied to companies which are operationally headquartered in very different societies. However, as Vedanta has listed its shares in London, it is reasonable that European-based investors who normally hold London-listed equities would apply consistent ethical standards to the company.

It is also worth noting that adherents of Hinduism would normally teach respect for the environment and communities, including sites such as the Niyamgiri hills, which have religious significance for the local community.

Drivers for short-term decision making

If ethical decision making is rational, and has some form of economic benefit, the reasons for unethical decision making need to be looked at carefully. One influence often cited is the drive for short-term performance. Trustees of investment funds, notably pension funds, typically focus on the last quarter's performance. This gives fund managers an incentive to focus on relatively short-term performance in their discussions with company management. However, the focus on short-term performance is typically balanced by also reviewing longer term performance figures, over for example a 5 year period. The backgrounds of trustees, and the level of training received can be very variable. Traded markets give immediate *liquidity* and price-signals for most major companies, enabling and sometimes requiring rapid decision making and implementation of decisions. At the same time, frequent trading has resulting costs, and is avoided by many successful investors. The efficiency of markets will reduce trading costs for investors who choose to trade at a given time, regardless of the rationale for trading, but does not give rise to an imperative to trade in normal circumstances.

CEOs of major companies typically have a perhaps surprisingly short tenure, of under five years. For many, this is their major opportunity to accumulate sometimes significant personal wealth. Equity-based incentives may align shareholders' interests with those of executives, but will only ever do so over specific timescales. One impact of longer term vesting of equity may well be to provide an incentive for CEOs to stay in post longer. This may in itself generally be positive, but at the same time will have its own unintended consequences.

It must be accepted that no set of incentives can be perfect, and that incentives do not explain all decisions. Some decisions can be mistakes, some self-aggrandising, some selfless, and some mistakenly attempting to be ethical. The management of Lehman's which led to its collapse cannot be attributed to a misalignment of incentives between shareholders and executives as the executives (notably CEO Richard Fuld) were major equity owners. Acquisitions can frequently appear to be as much about either ego of the acquiror's CEO, or the acquired CEO's desire to crystallise a significant amount of capital (or a combination of the two). Corporate decisions in reaction to criticism of ethical standards can have unfortunate consequences: according to Save the Children, the decision of one sporting goods manufacturer to pull out of manufacturing footballs in Bangladesh due to concerns over child labour led to much worse working conditions for the children concerned, rather than a reduction in abuse.

Quarterly reporting and earnings guidance

Especially in the US for companies with a stock market quote, there is a requirement to report earnings on a quarterly basis. This is also applicable to companies listed in other countries with a secondary US listing. It is conventional for US companies to also publish "earnings guidance." The aims of this include reducing the scope for individual analysts who cover the stock being in a privileged position by having access to the company to discuss their forecasts. One consequence is that companies can be penalised if they fail to meet short-term targets. The focus on short-term earnings has been criticised by some commentators and politicians for contributing to a short-term mentality in making decisions.

The failure to make correct decisions in complex circumstances will not have a single cause, including short-termism. Placing blame on short-term financial markets is superficial, given the complexity of markets. The adoption and use of an ethical decision framework could assist in some circumstances in considering broad issues when taking major or contentious decisions, but would be no guarantee that wrong decisions were not made.

Issues considered here include concerns about groups with strong long-term controlling investors – Vedanta, News International. There, management has substantial equity, and an unusually long-term approach to investment and value. There are sufficient examples of unethical decision making in very long-term businesses to query the extent to which short-termism is especially guilty of unusually driving unethical behaviour. Institutional investors in a quoted company are able to understand a complex strategy which offers benefits later – they backed the tech sector after all. However, they are also good at spotting trend lines – when performance starts to deteriorate, investors ask tough questions and some will vote with their feet.

4
Putting Business Ethics into Context

Lead us not into Temptation.

Matthew 6:13

Chapter summary

- Business does not exist in a vacuum. Low ethical standards in business are reflective of low ethical standards across society.
- Although bankers have been vilified widely for being especially corrupt, individuals from outside the banking or corporate sector have been shown to have had inadequate management judgement or personal ethics when appointed to roles in the banking sector.
- Ethical standards need to be thought through with sophistication, but be able to be explained in a tabloid form.
- Specific problems exist with mis-selling and misrepresentation across business sectors and across society, including in the new economy.
- The impact is seen as much in the public sector as in the private sector, across geographies and political allegiances.
- The short-term cost of ethical decisions, often seen in an opportunity cost, can be equated to the cost of an insurance premium. By implication, if the cost of the insurance looks excessive, then the risk is excessive.

Business does not exist in a vacuum. The majority of the working population in many countries, including the UK and the US, are employed by private enterprise.

Just as it is superficial to blame the financial crisis on a peculiar and particular moral turpitude among bankers, it is equally superficial to assume that business is peculiarly or intrinsically unethical and immoral. The well-publicised behaviour of Paul Flowers, a Chairman of a niche UK bank who came from outside the banking sector (he was a Methodist minister), demonstrates very clearly that banking is not unique in its corruption.

Sir Tom McKillop, who had enjoyed a very high reputation as Chief Executive of pharmaceutical company Astra Zeneca was Chairman of RBS at the time of its disastrous acquisition of ABN Amro. Although showing high standards of behaviour, he appears to have been unable to provide the type of challenge or guidance required by RBS, despite his success in another field of business.

Rajat Gupta, a Board member of Goldman Sachs and a former managing director of McKinsey was convicted on *insider trading* charges in June 2012 and received a two year prison sentence.

There are widespread instances and allegations of corrupt practices in fields as diverse as the provision of healthcare and fixing the results of sports matches.

The nature of ethical problems, risks and temptations will vary between businesses depending on their activities, and will be different from the problems, risks and temptations faced by the public sector and state-owned enterprises.

Ultimately, *business ethics* will more or less reflect the ethical standards of society as a whole. There is a tendency to criticise ethical failings in others, but to grasp temptation ourselves. This is not a distinctly modern trait, nor is it the preserve of any specific society, culture or country.

For business, ethical failings may lead to reputational damage, or long-term risks. This makes it important that businesses are able to define ethical standards, and set out frameworks to ask and answer questions about activities and contemplated activities. Of course, some companies will seek to profit by being actively (or relatively) unethical.

The standards of ethics and the understanding of ethics in professional firms which typically provide advice on the area needs to be understood in context. Professional ethics is a relatively narrow field, and relatively few lawyers have studies ethics as a separate discipline. According to Deborah Sabalot, a regulatory lawyer and editor of *Butterworths Securities and Financial Services Law Handbook,* the attempts through *regulation* of banks and investment banks to protect shareholders and companies from abuse remain "tick box" even after the reforms resulting from the financial crisis. Sabalot questions the role of legal firms in advising on reform of ethics and behaviour when a number "have major ethical problems themselves."

There is a strong argument that ethical policies must be able to be described in a simple tabloid manner – academic or legalistic language will make them unapproachable and distrusted by many stakeholders. This does not mean that the thinking around the ethical policies cannot or should not be complex, and their justification capable of being rigorously examined.

There is significant confusion over what constitutes "ethics" in business. An interesting example of this is looking at organisations seeking to increase their understanding of ethical issues. The qualifications sought when institutions are appointing internal *advisers* on ethics make little sense, effectively screening out anyone with a background actually in ethics. For example, when recruiting a Corporate Business Ethics Representative oil major Aramco stipulated qualifications should be a bachelor's degree in HR or a *compliance* related field. In 2014, UN agency UNESCO, seeking an Ethics Advisor, stipulated qualifications should include a degree level qualification in Law, Social Sciences, Public or Business Administration or a related discipline – rather surprisingly, these qualifications did not include ethics or moral philosophy, and effectively ruled out a candidate with an academic background or specialisation in ethics. These are not isolated examples, but are typical of an approach to ethics which is (at best) compliance driven, and highlight how corporations (and institutions) view ethics.

While banking in particular has been particularly excoriated for its standards, there have been clear examples of poor ethical standards in other major sectors: the Norwegian Pension Fund and the Church of England sold their shareholdings in Vedanta, a quoted mining company, due to the company's treatment of communities near to mining operations. The trial of a number of journalists including former editors of newspapers owned by News International has highlighted very poor standards, including hacking mobile phone messages in very contentious circumstances (this behaviour has already resulted in convictions in the UK courts).

There have also been extensive and wide-ranging investigations into the behaviour of the defence sector, including into how payments are made to intermediaries. The relatively recent UK Bribery Act brings the UK more into line with the US and the Foreign Corrupt Practices Act. However, there are some major international companies who believe (and behave accordingly) that an ability to be able to bribe effectively gives them a competitive advantage in some parts of the world.

Some of the worst examples of ethical breaches have been seen in contexts outside of the mainstream of business ethics, such as malfeasance over government and parliamentary expenses. In the UK, a MP claiming for maintenance of a "duck house" may have been farcical, but nonetheless indicates a standard of behaviour below the level society expects to be able to demand from politicians. The cover-up of safety issues or corruption of planning processes resulting in deaths from natural disaster is a prevalent theme in many countries, and endemic corruption at all levels has held back the development of a number of developing economies.

Ethics in business and society

Although problems with ethical standards seem to be prevalent, and the incentive or temptation to compromise ethical standards seems to be common, there is widespread negative reaction to exposure of unethical behaviour, especially among those with elected power, or with a high profile and a high income or significant personal wealth.

Consequently, there may be more merit in a successful company adopting high ethical standards to preserve shareholder value. This is both beneficial and problematic: beneficial, as it encourages the leading companies to set high standards; problematic, as it suggests that companies experiencing problems, not well known, or still small, might rationally set lower ethical standards (even where this is not publicly admitted) in order to be more successful. This could result in the relatively unethical proving successful at the expense of the ethical, which would be against the interests of their customers and society more generally. It is important to understand that the risk of this type of "free-ride" exists wherever the ethical bar is set: that is, the lower the bar, the more egregious the possible behaviour.

It is for this reason that in *Ethics in Investment Banking*, we argued that investment banks need to have both external regulation requiring ethical standards to be maintained, and industry-based self-regulation – external regulation will inevitably lag behind development in an industrial sector, but at the same time, some form of legal requirement is necessary to give the impetus for high standards of behaviour.

There are a number of areas in business and society where ethical standards are frequently seen to fail. Two of these with particular relevance to business are:

- Mis-selling: someone who has profited from misleading others, but not been caught, is often respected. There can be a very fine line between legal and illegal activity. It is important to be clear about the ethics of deliberately misleading when selling products and services. From an ethical perspective, misleading is the equivalent to lying. This may, in some cases, be very different from the difference between legal and illegal behaviour.
- Conflicts of interest: the openness about one's situation is important in this instance, but is not enough in a complex situation.

Although this book is about private sector business, it is worth noting that the dangers in this context faced by public sector organisations, individual politicians and political parties can be as great as for the private sector:

- New York state governor Eliot Spitzer resigned in the wake of a prostitution scandal in 2008. In 1998, President Clinton's relationship with Monica Lewinsky was the cause of impeachment proceedings (of which he was subsequently acquitted).
- The level of public concern over the attempt to vilify UK politician Andrew Mitchell by the Police Federation showed dishonesty in an elite section of the supposedly apolitical British police. This showed that ethical lapses can easily extend significantly beyond private companies. The response to the scandal from the Commissioner of the Metropolitan Police – backing the police officers and then subsequently apologising to Mr Mitchell raised serious questions about the police's approach to their role and due process.

- The membership of the constituency Labour Party in Falkirk in Scotland was found to have been artificially inflated by members of the Unite trade union in 2012, some of whom apparently did not realise they had joined the party, in order to elect a chosen candidate to replace Eric Joyce, a Member of Parliament who resigned after being arrested for assaulting people in a bar.
- Silvio Berlusconi, controlling shareholder of media group Mediaset and former Italian premier, was convicted in 2013 of tax evasion, and was the subject of allegations of impropriety at notorious "Bunga Bunga" parties and of using an underage prostitute.
- In China, the problems of corruption are sufficiently widespread that criminals convicted of crimes such as embezzlement can be sentenced to capital punishment (and there are some complex sentences available to Chinese courts, such as a death sentence with a two year reprieve). The 2008 infant formula milk scandal saw a number of convictions, with an estimated 300,000 people affected.
- The award of the soccer world cup by FIFA to Qatar, a country where temperatures can be c. 40 centigrade in summer, has been surrounded in controversy, with allegations of payments to FIFA officials and their families.
- In July 2007, BBC children's TV programme "Blue Peter" was fined £50,000 for faking the result of a TV phone in (using premium rate phone lines), and making a child complicit in pretending to be a competition winner.

Standards of ethics in business do not appear to be out of kilter with standards in society more generally (sadly). It is difficult to find a sector of society, or a geographic region, which has not seen significant ethical shortcomings, even in those areas where high standards would be most expected and required.

There is not a simple or obvious correlation between the ethical issues:

- covered in the media, and the subject of political focus;
- the focus of companies' *CSR* Reports;
- the focus of attention by ethical investors.

Companies will be cognisant of the damage which can be caused by adverse media and political comment, and spend sometimes significant sums managing their press and political relations. The media and political focus tends to be on very populist issues, and on those which receive political comment (such as tax payments and anti-competitive behaviour). In some cases, company directors may be more attentive to articles in high profile media than to extensive discussions internally within their companies. Although ethical standards in society change over time, companies seeking to develop and maintain long-term strategies will need to adopt sets of values which are capable of withstanding long-term scrutiny.

Company reports on CSR and related issues seem to be read by relatively narrow audiences (including specialist investors, single-issue lobbying groups and journalists) and are largely in response to external codes of conduct. Ethical investors have varying subjects of especial interest, often trying to look at underlying issues, and often ahead of the codes of conduct and resulting company reports. This suggests a difference in the understanding of the nature of ethics between the different constituents, as well as a different set of premises underlying their focus. For example, ethical investors are concerned about the level of activity undertaken by retailing groups in the areas of alcohol, gambling and pornography (the latter two over mobile phones and similar technology), but the CSR Reports of Tesco, Sainsbury and Walmart do not give any indication of the level of sales from these activities. The Tesco and Society Report 2013[1] covers some key issues such as food waste and local communities, but does not address for example the issues underlying concerns expressed by ethical investors, including the aggregate level of sales of alcohol, gambling products (lottery tickets), tobacco and pornography (via mobile phone downloads). Walmart, which has been frequently subject to criticism over some its practices including employment practices, publishes a substantial "Global Responsibility Report," which includes reference to core values of integrity, opportunity, family and community, purpose and responsibility[2] but again doesn't move outside its set areas into more challenging territory.

Ethical and CSR focused investors will typically take as a starting point for their activities the identification of sectors in which they do not wish to invest. Very few companies seem to acknowledge the ethical validity of this approach – this is especially surprising as ethically focused investors from a very wide variety of cultures and countries have the same range of ethical concerns to a very (and surprisingly) large extent.

In summary, the media and political focus is on issues with a popular currency, which may not be clear-cut in terms of business implications. CSR Reports in the main – and there are notable exceptions, both positive and negative – are responsive, and tend to relate to external codes of practice. In this case, the report may simply "report" on activity, rather than reflect corporate priorities. Ethical investors in the main are focused on agendas set by their founding premises, which can vary: some investment funds focus on environmental issues, others have complex ethical frameworks derived from a theological perspective, including Jewish, Islamic and from various Christian denominations. These latter are rarely reflected directly in corporate codes of practice, which tend to be much more legalistic in approach, and rather miss the thrust of much of the ethical debate:

> *There is a mismatch between the expectation of others being ethical and the behaviours which we expect to follow ourselves (this is nothing new – see the parable of the Good Samaritan). Ethics as an academic study is atomised and complex. One reason for the mismatch is the divergent and irreconcilable set of ethical principles underlying free markets on the one side and socialism on the other, making a single set of ethics impossible to identify. Companies, and society, need to be able to follow and be judged by straightforward ethical rules.*

The cost of ethics

In the short term at least, ethical discussion-making may present a cost to a business and its shareholders. This can be compared and contrasted with the way in which obeying the law also presents an opportunity cost.

There is a major difference between corporate attitudes to criminal law and to contract law. For example, a company may determine that the penalties associated with a breach of contract are acceptable rather than obeying a contract. This may be effectively a contractual right, but attitudes to this type of breach vary between countries. Such an approach might be expected more in the US than in Europe, for example. A contractual obligation with a penalty associated can be seen as a choice for a company, or as a moral obligation. Contract clauses can prove to be different in litigation than expected when they are signed, although it is not always clear if both sides are subject to the same level of surprise at how clauses are interpreted in court. The difference in approach to *subordinated debt* has given opportunities to junior creditors in Europe to receive greater value in restructurings than would have been identified by *senior debt* holders, in part through exercising contractual rights to agree to the *restructuring* of debt. There is an ethical issue here: if a company felt it should abide by the spirit of a contract, it might miss out on benefits from litigating over its full contractual rights, thereby depriving shareholders of value. However, at the same time it could be taking advantage of an error in the agreement reached between two companies when it was set in writing.

Different companies operating in the same sector can have strong and contrasting cultures – in fact, this is frequently the case. While from the outside they may appear to be similar in that they carry out similar activities, the way they do business and act can be meaningfully varied. This type of variation can survive through successive generations of leaderships, as strong corporate values can be sought in those selected from succession to the most senior roles. This type of cultural difference can lead different companies to respond differently to questions which may have ethical connotations. Some banks managed to avoid the worst problems of the financial crisis through having actively avoided involvement in some of the most damaging securities involved. Others were too slow moving to embrace the opportunity, and avoided problems through an inability to enter the new markets. Both cultures may have subsequently been seen as successful, although one success was based on largely ethical considerations, the other was not.

For an investor, ethics reduces the range of investment options open, and therefore will either increase the risk of investment or reduce the *returns*. This is based on the assumption of the **option value** of being able to choose between a greater range of potential investments or activities. As the universe of ethical investors grows, two things could happen: first, it is possible that the available return on unethical investments would increase, making them relatively more attractive; second, that unethical investments could become increasingly publicly and politically unpalatable, ultimately making them illegal and therefore very risky. In the case of proscribed drugs, both these eventualities appear to have happened.

Conversely, a number of major scandals have demonstrated poor ethical standards at the company affected, which have contributed to ultimately damaging behaviour. Comparison of ethical failings with ethical costs is difficult. There are arguments that many major corporate failures are preceded by periods of "hubris," where company management acts as if they believe they are virtually infallible:

> *Ethics has a potential cost, which may in the short term have no off-setting benefit. At the same time, this cost can be seen as being equivalent to an insurance premium, protecting the long-term interests and value of a business and its shareholders. Companies which would not skimp on paying an insurance premium should not be expected to balk at using an ethical framework to protect the interest of shareholders.*

5

Applying Business Ethics

He who fights with monsters should look to it that he does not also become a monster. And when he gazes long into an abyss, the abyss also gazes back.

Friedrich Nietzsche (1844–1900),
Beyond Good and Evil (1886)

Chapter summary

- There is a longstanding attempt by moral philosophers to set out the principles by which individuals should behave and by which governments should act in the interests of citizens.
- Much ethical thinking predates the idea of a global company, and concepts which are used must be carefully considered in order to be applied reasonably and fairly.
- Key ethical concepts – justice and fairness – determine who has ethical rights regarding a company's behaviour, and to whom it owes ethical duties.
- Ethical concepts may appear to be in conflict, especially in relation to shareholder rights versus equality and inequality.
- The traditions of duty-based, virtue and consequentialist ethics all have lessons for business leaders.
- It is important to be aware of the danger of consequentialist thinking leading to moral-relativism, which can be used to justify otherwise damaging actions.
- Attempts to develop more equality-based alternatives to capitalism have foundered, at least as much in practice as in theory.

- Capitalism, for all its flaws, may remain the most effective means of describing a fair way of managing relationships between individuals, companies and governments.
- Globalisation is a phenomenon, not a movement or a conspiracy.
- The hoped-for democratising effect of social media and distributed content provision has not materialised into an ethically superior new society.
- The considered thoughts of business leaders on ethics can also be instructive.

Ethicists and philosophers have sought to apply ethical thinking to real-life situations, with differing conclusions, drawing on established schools of ethical thinking.

Adam Smith in his *Theory of Moral Sentiments* adopts an approach which is close in some key aspects to Aristotelian virtue ethics, arguing that virtue needs to be adopted, but also accepting the requirement for and existence of some underlying moral rules.

Among the most influential recent contributions to our understanding of ethics is John Rawls' theory of justice. Rawls sets out a "difference" principle, which argues that social and economic imbalances are acceptable provided that they work to the benefit of the most disadvantaged. Rawls argues that inequality is acceptable, provided it can be justified. This suggests that equality of outcome is not per se ethically required in considering remuneration.

Gerald Cohen in *Rescuing Justice and Equality*[1] develops an argument that Rawls is too forgiving of inequality. He argues that we could analyse how we would behave in an unequal and incentivised society, and act in the same way without the incentives.

Kant shows that in his theory of ethics, the state should exercise a duty to the common good, including a duty to the poor.[2]

Philosopher and novelist Ayn Rand provokes significant controversy, but has a particular relevance to understanding decision making in business contexts, and has been influential especially in the US. Rand's Objectivist philosophy argues in favour of capitalism and high levels of personal freedom, to the extent of considering altruism as being immoral, in that it undermines personal freedom. Rand has been criticised extensively for the extent of her support for freedom over other ethical values (e.g. justice).

Much of this thinking predates the modern concept of a global company, and therefore cannot be expected to address specifically some of the complex issues – such as internet based marketing – which are prevalent today. The language of *business ethics* is confused – ethical thinking has largely diverged from the language of the corporate world since the mid-20th century, and ethical thinking surrounding business needs to be fundamentally reassessed, to take account of the context of business decisions in a global market, to take account of the impact of modern technology (internet based marketing), and to take account of the lag in the development of the commercial arena with the policy of governments.

It is possible to consider and apply ethical principles to inform decision making. Ethics of government are also relevant for major companies, given the range of impact that corporate decision making can have:

> In order for a business to understand the ethical implications of its decisions, it needs to have a framework which can help identify ethical issues arising from the major ethical traditions: duty, virtue and consequences. However, in practical terms a judgement will often need to be made between two fundamentally conflicting concerns: freedom (and the rights of shareholders) and justice (and the duty to support government/society).

The main traditions of moral philosophy can provide a framework for business ethics. There are areas of uncertainty in many practical situations, in part because it is not always possible to fully understand a complex situation, and in part because of areas of uncertainty and sometimes disagreement between the different ethical traditions.

There are three main approaches to moral philosophy in western traditions: *deontological* or duty-based, assessing the moral rules and duties we have towards each other; *consequentialist* or *utilitarian*, assessing the consequences or collective benefit of our actions; and *virtue*, developing patterns of good or virtuous behaviour.[3] Ultimately, consequentialist ethics can prove difficult in practice, as ethical arguments can be adduced to justify behaviour which under other standards looks unethical. A focus on duties (and rights), and also on virtue may offer the most likely prospect of developing a satisfactory ethical framework for corporate decision making.

Ethical traditions and concepts which have been developed separately from the western traditions, for example in India, China and

Japan – such as *Dharma* – are also useful in considering how to make decisions.

Decision making for a large company has an impact on a very wide group of people. As well as looking at ethical teaching, it is also useful to look at the ethics of government decision making and the social contract. This is particularly relevant when considering questions of taxation, but also has a significant influence on questions of remuneration.

Duty-based (deontological)

Duty-based ethics can be used to construct a useable framework for corporate decision making. Taking its name from *deos*, the Greek word for duty, deontological ethics is based on the principle that there are universal moral "duties" that should be used to determine how we behave. In this school of ethical thought, it is what we do and why which is important, rather than the consequences of our actions.

Duty-based ethics has its basis in the concept of "natural law," the belief that there is a universal moral code which should be followed. Both Aristotle (384–322 BCE) and the Christian theologian and philosopher Thomas Aquinas (1225–74) argued that there is a universal moral code which is central to leading a "good life."

Natural law is developed both in classical philosophy, and a theological belief that the moral structure of the world can be understood through divine revelation and therefore understood through reason. A belief in natural law can be seen in the Wisdom literature of the Jewish scriptures, and is expressed in Christianity, for example in Paul's letter to the Romans (2:15) where what is required to live a good life is "written on their hearts, to which their own conscience also bears witness."

The German philosopher Immanuel Kant (1724–1804) made a major contribution to ethical thinking. Of particular note, he developed the idea of a "categorical imperative," an ethical rule which can never be justifiably violated. Although this is perhaps not the most sophisticated concept in term of modern ethical thinking, it can be used helpfully in developing applied ethical frameworks, and has the advantage of clarity and simplicity. To Kant, deontological ethics provides a comprehensive structure for behaviour and decision making, and "a conflict of duties is inconceivable." This approach has been criticised by Bernard Williams, who introduced the idea of "moral luck" in challenging the ability to identify specific moral value associated with actions.

Virtue ethics

Originating with the Greek philosopher Plato (428/427–348/347 BCE) and developed by Thomas Aquinas "the Disposition to act well," virtue ethics is based on the concept of achieving ethical behaviour by identifying and practising performing virtuous acts.

The idea of virtue ethics is that there are desirable human behaviours which naturally work to promote that which is good. Virtuous behaviours cannot be seen in isolation from ethical behaviour because it is by acting ethically over and over again that virtuous habits are developed, and it is by developing virtuous habits that we are more likely to act ethically – the two are inextricably linked and inevitably interact.

Virtue ethics has an important implication for business: this school of thinking suggests that ethical decision making can be learned through practise, and (unlike duty-based ethics), is not simply based on reason. This has clear implications for a company seeking to provide an ethical framework which is effective for large numbers of employees. It also implies that an organisation cannot be "ethical" if ethics are not a part of the overall conduct of the organisation, rather than a separate "screen" applied by a Board (or other) committee.

Consequentialist

Contrasting with duty-based ethics, the basis of this school of ethics is that it is necessary to consider the most desirable outcome when making a decision, rather than moral absolutes.

The best-known form of consequentialism is utilitarianism, which is most associated with Jeremy Bentham (1748–1832) and John Stuart Mill (1806–1873). Utilitarianism provides the basis for much economic thinking, where utility maximisation is a key guiding principle. Utilitarianism lends itself to quantification, enabling ethical criteria to be applied practically, for example in a cost-benefit analysis.

Consequentialist ethics has the benefit of being practical, and being able to be applied in complex situations, whereas duty- or virtue-based ethics can become complex or impractical. However, consequentialism and utilitarianism face two particular problems: first, in quantification – how can the greatest good be calculated – and second, that it can lead to outcomes which are by other standards clearly unethical.

The complexity of understanding consequences can include both multiple factors and unpredictability. In business, as in life, sometimes even simple decisions have unintended consequences.

Despite criticisms levelled at it, consequentialist and utilitarian ethics remain an important if incomplete branch of moral philosophy. Assessing moral outcomes is an important part of ethical decision making. This can be consistent with the natural law approach to ethics, in which there is an inherent understanding that it is right to act in a way that maximises that which is good.

Attempting to reconcile ethical concepts

In reconciling conflicts between duties, it is useful to look at another important element of Kant's thinking, that regarding personal freedom. In *Metaphysics of Morals* Kant argues that "right is the restriction of each individual's freedom so that it harmonises with the freedom of everyone else."[4] A focus on personal freedom is not itself uncontentious. Giles Fraser writing in the *Guardian* (20 September 2013) said "From the mid 20th century onwards, freedom has become the west's dominant morality – freedom from fascism, free trade, free love, free speech. But when we seek freedom from the things that bind us together, then we are not free. We are lost." Critics of the priority given to freedom over equality are themselves subject to challenge – it may be the case that it is easy to say freedom is overstated if you have it.

For a number of theologians and philosophers, freedom has been an important criteria of what constitutes an ethical action or decision. The Christian theologian and bishop, Augustine of Hippo, took free bargaining as being essential in agreeing wages, based on New Testament teaching.

The debate between justice and freedom is of paramount importance in the application of ethics to corporate decision making. The precepts of both arguments – from both a religious and secular perspective – cannot always be easily reconciled (if at all).

Within duty-based ethics, the question of justice is prominent. An influential contemporary theory of justice which has been applied to economics is that developed by the philosopher John Rawls. Rawls' theory of justice centres on two principles which can be used to determine whether or not an action is just. Rawls' first principle of justice is that each person is to have an equal right to the most extensive scheme of equal basic liberties compatible with a similar scheme of liberties for others. Rawls' second principle is that inequalities should be arranged such that (i) they are to be of the greatest benefit to the least-advantaged members of society, and (ii) that there is equality of opportunity in terms of employment.

The first principle focuses on universal human rights, to ensure that basic freedoms are available to everyone affected by a decision. The second acknowledges that inequalities are inevitable in a society that is free and where there is competition. However, for reasons of equity (rather than equality) an economic or business decision is just: (i) only if those who benefit least from it are still better off than they would be had that decision not been taken, and (ii) only if there is equality of opportunity in terms of employment (so that, in theory at least, all could gain the maximum benefit).

Different ideas of duty

It should be borne in mind that the concept of duty varies between philosophical and cultural traditions. Kant wrote from the perspective of "reason," and did not base his treatment of ethics purely on religious arguments, although some would see the appeal to "natural law" as implicitly religious. The Hindu concept of *Dharma* which is often translated as duty is more akin to the formal idea of duty found in the Stoics or Cicero than in some later philosophy such as Rawls. Dharma is the concept of fulfilling one's duty according to invariable natural laws, and traditionally implies a duty to follow the role according to one's caste, but can also be interpreted as providing a means to live a fulfilling life without pursuit of material wealth or power. In the Hindu epic poem, the "Mahabharata," the Pandavas represent the idea of Dharma. Confusion should be avoided in comparing the concept of Dharma in Hinduism with its use in Buddhism. In general, Dharma in Buddhism has different connotations (the path taught by Buddha, following the natural laws of the universe), and does not equate directly to duty as it does in Hinduism.

Differences between the US and Europe

There are surprising differences in ethics and moral philosophy between Europe (probably including the UK) and North America. The Christian-democracy and social-democracy which has been a major force and influence in Europe has had significantly less influence in the US, whereas the US has continued a more laissez-faire approach to economic and welfare issues. Empirically, the US has delivered a higher standard of living since 1945, although it is not straightforward to assign this only to specific factors such as differences in employee mobility – there are differences in natural resources, for example, which are considered to have an impact on levels of growth. The US approach to ethical questions has been influenced by relatively (compared to Europe and Asia) recent history. The foundation of the US Constitution was strongly influenced by European Protestants, and later by Jewish immigrants, and this is reflected in the approach to business ethics seen in the US.

Attitudes of the faiths

Despite sometimes surprising differences, the Catholic Church and the Anglican denominations have a similar approach to their view of ethical problems arising from the financial crisis. Leaders of both churches have argued that the financial and commercial world is not distinct from other areas of human interaction. Pope Benedict XVI, in the *encyclical Caritas in Veritate* (29 January 2009), stated that "Every economic decision has a moral consequence" (para. 37). Rowan Williams, then Archbishop of Canterbury said in a speech at Trinity Church on Wall Street in 2010 that economic activity "is subject to the same moral considerations as all other activities."

It is interesting to note, by comparison, that many central bankers have not seen ethics as a core part of the problems facing banking.

In countries with diverse ethnic and cultural traditions, an understanding of ethics will include appreciating the diversity of understanding of key cultural concepts.

Shariah financing – a growing and now important part of the finance markets – is based on predominant western forms of financing, adjusted for the tenets of Shariah law. This is feasible in part due to the common background of the *Abrahamic faiths*: Islam, Christianity and Judaism. Some cultures will find acceptable ethical practices in one culture to be morally repellent – to take a simple example, it would be considered to be immoral to eat pork in Tel Aviv or Riyadh. The punishments for theft under Shariah law could include amputation, which would be considered unethical in most (if not all) modern western democracies. Many western countries do not share the moral requirements for charitable giving found in Islam, which may or may not be satisfied in national or local tax regimes.

The growth of Shariah financing could lead to changes in the financing markets, given the Shariah requirement to share risk, and its prohibition on interest payments.

Duties of, and to, government and the social contract

The issue of political or social ethics stems from much of the same thinking as we can use as a basis for business ethics. One key principle we can also turn to is that of a "social contract." This concept, developed in the Enlightenment, is particularly associated with the French philosopher Jean-Jacques Rousseau (1712–1778). Under a "social contract," individuals consent to give up some of their rights to government in order that government can protect their remaining rights. Thomas Hobbes (1588–1679) argued that people give up their rights to the absolute authority of government.

Hobbes wrote in *Leviathan* that:

> The Kingdom of darkness...is nothing else but a confederacy of deceivers that, to obtain dominion over men in this present world, endeavour, by dark and erroneous doctrines, to extinguish in them the light. (Hobbes, *Leviathan*, ch. XLIV)

Hobbes argues that without government, people would exist in the "state of nature" and there would be "bellum omnia contra omnes" (all would be in a war against all).

John Locke (1632–1709) argued that an individual's rights are inalienable (and superseded by the laws of God) and that each person has such rights in a natural state:

> To properly understand political power and trace its origins, we must consider the state that all people are in naturally. That is a state of perfect freedom of acting and disposing of their own possessions and persons as they think fit within the bounds of the law of nature. People in this state do not have to ask permission to act or depend on the will of others to arrange matters on their behalf. The natural state is also one of equality in which all power and jurisdiction is reciprocal and no one has more than another. It is evident that all human beings – as creatures belonging to the same species and rank and born indiscriminately with all the same natural advantages and faculties – are equal amongst themselves. They have no relationship of subordination or subjection unless God (the lord and master of them all) had clearly set one person above another and conferred on him an undoubted right to dominion and sovereignty. (Two Treatises on Government: A Translation into Modern English, *ISR/Google Books*, 2009)

Locke was writing to support the accession of William of Orange to the throne (a polarizing figure), and his ideas were also influential in the foundation of the United States.

Kant further developed the idea of natural law and is also influential in developing the concept of the social contract. He stated that the civil state is based on three *a priori* principles: freedom, equality and independence. Kant argues that the welfare of citizens cannot be the basis of a state's power. His argument is that freedom is an inalienable right, so long as it does not conflict with anyone else's freedom:

> Any action is right if it can coexist with everyone's freedom in accordance with a universal law, or if on its maxim the freedom of choice of each can coexist with everyone's freedom in accordance with a universal law. (*Metaphysics of Morals*)

Kant specifically challenges the idea that the state should seek to make its citizens happy, arguing that happiness is too vague a concept to be a valid goal for a government.

In *Theory and Practice*, Kant sets out three principles underlying the state:

- The freedom of every member of the state as a human being.
- The equality of each with every other as a subject.
- The independence of every member of a commonwealth or state as a citizen.

The concept of equality is one of equality before the law, and does not equate to equality of income, wealth, position and so on, but more closely to equality of opportunity.

Both Kant and Hobbes considered that the sovereign (or government) derives power from a social contract, and that the social contract was not a historic fact, but a rational condition to exist. As such, the social contract can in a sense be imposed on citizens regardless of their choice, as according to Kant "free will" equates to practical reason, and practical reason dictates acceptance of the social contract. There are important differences between the views taken by Kant and Hobbes. These include Hobbes' view that each individual should benefit from the social contract, whereas Kant bases his argument on freedom in general for citizens, not just for each individual.

In *Du contrat social ou Principes du droit politique* (1762) Rousseau considered whether government could be legitimate, and what forms of government had legitimacy. He argued that only popular will gave the legitimacy to legislate. Freedom is universal, because people give up the same rights (to government) and have the same duties. Rousseau also argued that freedom is best protected by small city states (he was a citizen of Geneva, at that time a canton or city-state).

The idea of a social contract is challenged by a number of ethical arguments advanced by (among others) Hegel (based on equality) and John Stuart Mill (based on consequences), and also by communism and the thinking of, for example, Marx. In particular, there are arguments that the primacy of freedom understates the importance of equality and justice.

In his *A Theory of Justice*, John Rawls attempted to reconcile the clash between freedom and equality through "fairness." Rawls argued that there are two ethical principles, those of liberty and equality, which should be ordered so that an individual's rights can't be subsumed by the demands of equality, but that issues of equality are not ignored. Rawls hypothesised a situation where individuals under "a veil of ignorance" would agree to certain premises of justice and legal organisation. Rawls' idea of justice specifically allows inequality of resources.

Rawls' theory of justice is not without criticism. US philosopher Robert Nozick (1938–2002) argued that it had a number of flaws, including the inability to systematically define the process required to make ethical decisions, and that inequality of result could not be taken to imply injustice. Nevertheless, both Nozick and Rawls appear to argue that utilitarianism risks ignoring the rights of an individual, setting no absolute individual rights which cannot be overridden.

It is the nature of philosophy and ethics that debate and thinking continues to develop.

The social contract and limited liability

Most companies of any size are "limited liability" legal entities. They are recognised under the law, and therefore able to enter into contracts in their own right and litigate in their own name. The risk taken by shareholders is limited to the level of equity subscribed – in the event of insolvency, creditors are (normally) unable to seek personal restitution from shareholders and directors. Such companies allow capital to be efficiently raised and cycled through the economy. These companies are only feasible in the environment of (relatively) stable government and rule of law. The existence and maintenance of limited liability is a part of the modern social contract, and one from which significant obligations fall on both companies and shareholders.

The concept of a social contract does not set out the limitations of the relationship between the individual and the state, but rather it rationalises the relationship. The principle of limited liability depends on the legal system, and therefore the state, which in turn depends on the consent (express or implied) of individuals, including individuals when acting as shareholders. The interaction between individual, state and company is complex, and should not be seen in an antagonistic sense, as it is through individuals that the state has authority, and through the state that companies can operate and grow.

Society, equality and capitalism

This book has argued that business ethics reflect the ethics more prevalent in society. In *Ethics in Investment Banking*, we sought to demonstrate that the failings and structures leading to the financial crisis reflected those in industry and commerce more widely: mis-selling is prevalent rather than unusual, look at the "aspirational" adverts for cars or the sales practices in real estate. Compare the implicit government support for banks with that in many countries for the car industry or for utilities.

As capitalism has developed, and philosophical thinking has changed, so has appreciation and criticism of capitalism, influenced by the growth in understanding of both economics and sociology. Capitalism has been criticised for the levels of inequality that it produces, and for the character traits it may encourage (greed). While outright criticisms of capitalism struggle to develop an alternative that does not oppress individual freedoms, at the same time many argue that capitalism requires *regulation* and therefore the existence of strong government in order to be successful.

Georg Hegel (1770–1831) in *Elements of the Philosophy of Right* developed the concept of the "Sittlichkeit" or Ethical Life. In this concept, it is the ownership of property that grants rights. Hegel believed that markets need to be tempered by the type of consciousness found in family relationships.

Thomas Piketty in *Capital in the Twenty First Century* argues that inequality will increase when savings from current remuneration cannot grow at as high a rate as accumulated wealth. According to Piketty the accumulation of wealth "becomes more rapid and inegalitarian as the return on capital rises and the growth rate falls." "Whenever the rate of return on capital is significantly and durably higher than the growth rate of the economy, it is all but inevitable that inheritance (of fortunes accumulated in the past) predominates over saving (wealth accumulated in the present)."

This alternative interpretation of modern capitalism has divided views in Europe and the US. It offers a clear rationale for government policy to address inequality. At the same time, it does not seem to fully allow for risk in investment decisions (inherited wealth can be invested at low *returns* as well as high). Nor does its central thesis allow for the impact of disruptive technology to reduce the value of long established business models.

Government action, inaction and policy, both nationally and internationally may also contribute to inequality. Lottery winners are not taxed, which contributes to inequality of outcome, but the lottery is supported by parties of a wide spectrum of beliefs in a wide range of countries. One result of the criminalisation of drugs has been the creation of a relatively widespread relatively wealthy class of criminals, and an increase in inequality of wealth and outcome in parts of society where inequality may be associated both with crime as well as with celebrity or business success.

If it is not the prerogative of a company to have regard to managing social problems directly, it is the prerogative of government. A company will require stability to operate – maintain good employee relations, recruit educated staff and so on – and that requires a highly stable society. Consequently, it is reasonable for a company through its support for a society, from paying taxes and taking into account elements of popular sentiment, to "support" measures necessary to maintain good social order. This may include both progressive taxation, and elements of redistribution, if this is required to prevent inequality becoming a cause of, for example, civil unrest.

Inequality and relative poverty – the context

There are a wide range of ethical reasons for both poverty and equality being important issues. It is difficult to tolerate widespread abuse, disease and hunger. These problems are exacerbated by inequality, which can take hope and prospects for development away from whole communities for more than one generation.

Many NGOs define extreme poverty as living on less than $1 per day, a level of income which generally resonates in the developed world. There are also arguments that *relative* poverty, even in relatively wealthy countries, is a social ill: living on an income in the bottom quartile whatever the income may be will restrict opportunity. Consequently, based on this argument both absolute and relative inequality can be considered to be social ills, and contributing to them is therefore unethical behaviour.

For many people, the obvious reference points of wealth inequality are not the most wealthy (*hedge fund* managers, business owners) but the highest profile (sports stars, actors, well recognised personalities). (Try asking someone standing outside a subway station in a rundown

London or New York district to name someone rich: they won't name a hedge fund manager. Then ask them who the richest person they themselves know is. It's salutary). In addition, in many depressed communities the closest point of reference to wealth may also be serious criminals, including people who deal drugs.

Attempts to specifically equate executive remuneration to causes of chronic inequality are not sufficiently convincing to justify Boards of companies altering their behaviour to treat relative inequality as a priority.

As an example, it is important to look at the causes of social unrest. The Occupy movement did a lot to expand awareness of public anger at the way the financial bail-out operated, and at growing inequality. Although the Occupy movement was in direct response to ongoing inequality and notably the foreclosure of mortgages and the banking bail-outs, the executives responsible for the financial crisis had already been paid. The Occupy movement, which originated in 2011, used the slogan "we are the 99%" protesting against inequality, and the undue influence of major companies (particularly banks) on government. In the main, where there have been large scale protests and riots they have been based on violations of civil rights rather than expressions regarding inequality per se: riots in Turkey in 2014 about safety conditions and the government response to a mining disaster in Soma; the riots in 2011 in London and other UK cities were in result of the shooting by armed police of Mark Duggan in Tottenham, northeast London. Most of the rioters did not know the victim of the shooting. Egregious as it was to many shareholders (especially small shareholders), the proposed remuneration of Barclays employees in 2014 did not bring people onto the streets of London. Other examples of major civil unrest have been less obviously focused on issues such as inequality. In France in 2005, widespread rioting in the banlieus (suburbs) around Paris were started following the accidental electrocution of two teenagers who were hiding from police in an electricity sub-station. The riots spread to many areas of France, with a particular feature being cars set alight (around 9,000 in total). A number of fundamental causes have been suggested in both France and the UK for the riots, including disaffected youth with little hope for the future. In 2014, there were riots in Brazil over evictions from the favelas to allow construction for the football world cup. It is overstating the case for equality, or against inequality, to imply that increasing wealth inequality is an extreme issue dividing society. Social cohesion and social unrest are issues which relate to a much broader spectrum of causes than wealth inequality, with racism and problems of integration probably significant causes. Mass protests in the UK have been held over issues such as the poll tax (local taxes), the Iraq war and the ban on fox-hunting. Relative poverty in Europe or the US, when compared with, for example, Kazakhstan, Angola or Nigeria becomes a much less meaningful issue. It is important to ask, when considering measures to address this, how globally efforts to address poverty and inequality should be focused?

Challenging and defending capitalism

Capitalism has been challenged by many philosophers and writers, notably by socialist thinking. Hegel's *Elements of the Philosophy of Right* sets out the concept that free will can only be expressed in the context of a complex series of relationships including property rights, ethical ties, family life, the legal system and government. Hegel's historicist and idealist philosophy formed the basis of Marxism, a form of socialism. The basic premise of socialism is that the means of production should be controlled by workers, who are best placed to make decisions about their activities, and without exploitation by outside owners of capital, will benefit from (various forms of) collective ownership. Marx and Engels played a major role in developing communist and socialist thinking, which was both critical of capitalism and also proposed alternatives. Karl Marx (1818–1883) argued that society develops through class struggle – a struggle between owners of material wealth and a dispossessed class of workers. Marx believed that profits were created from the unacknowledged value of labour, and that capitalism would inevitably collapse and ultimately give rise to a communist system of government. Marx saw capitalism as of limited endurance, not as an enduring economic, social or philosophical phenomenon. In *Das Kapital*, Marx set out his view – based on an analysis of economic history – that the economic crises inevitable in capitalism would give rise to a socialist revolution. Marx developed an understanding of history which led him to conclude that there was an alternative (or, he would argue, successor) to capitalism, which might (in some countries) require revolution. The basic concept that surplus profits are derived from exploitation of labour is more difficult to consider in the internet age, where global businesses can be built very quickly, and "labour" is not always a major input. Having said that, there is much of what Marx would recognise as exploitation of labour in the production of many modern consumer goods.

In much socialist thinking, capitalism oppresses labour, depriving workers of their freedom. Freedom is of great importance to Marx and in other socialist philosophy, equating to both freedom of opportunity and freedom to use the resources that an individual requires. The argument for this type of freedom is made both by secular thinkers, such as Marx, and also by ethicists from religious traditions.

Max Weber (1864–1920) gave rise to the later concept of the work ethic in *The Protestant Ethic and the Spirit of Capitalism*. Here, Weber sets out the basis for how we see work and economic activity, with the role of work having progressed from being viewed as a puritan (or Protestant) virtue, to being a necessity: "the essential elements of the attitude which was there called the spirit of capitalism are the same as what we have just shown to be the content of the Puritan worldly asceticism, only without the religious basis." Weber is known as one of the developers of sociology as a science, and argued that society has to be understood by looking at the actions of individuals. For Weber, unlike Marx, capitalism is very much imperfect, but is to be understood as an explanation of activity, rather than fought. Where Marx views the economic "base" of society as the determining influence of society as a whole, Weber sees capitalism as emerging from the work ethic, which has its origin in Protestant thinking. However, Weber accepts but remains critical of capitalism's focus on material goods: likening a focus on material goods to being in an "iron cage," Weber concludes that "victorious capitalism... needs the support of religion no longer."

Ayn Rand set out one of the staunchest and most contentious defences of capitalism in *Atlas Shrugged* (a novel) and in *Capitalism: The Unknown Ideal* (described as a non-fiction footnote to her novel *Atlas Shrugged*). Rand, perhaps best known for developing the idea of "objectivism" states that "Capitalism is the only system geared to the life of a rational being and the only *moral* politico-economic system in history." Rand argues that "Those who advocate laissez-faire capitalism are the only advocates of man's rights," and denies that other forms of collective rights exist. Rand's views are in contradiction to those of Marx, and to some extent reflect the thinking of earlier philosophers, including Rousseau and Kant, that government exists because it is given power to do so by individuals, who choose to cede certain rights to a government, in order that the government may protect their remaining rights.

Glasnost, the events of 1989, and some economic liberalism in China have all contributed to an acceptance that some forms of socialism, notably state-socialism, have proven unworkable. The financial crisis starting in 2007–08 led a significant number of commentators to consider that the benefits of capitalism were not clear cut, and that markets may have either failed or been shown to be systematically dysfunctional.

The growth in income inequality has been cited as a reason for increasing civil unrest, and as a cause and source of social injustice. Income inequality was a major stated reason behind the Occupy movement's activities, and has been a notable feature of political debate, especially in the US, where the impact of taxes has been less progressive than in other OECD countries, according to a number of studies.

In November 2013, Pope Francis in *Evangelii Gaudium* (The Joy of the Gospel) stated that:

> [U]ntil exclusion and inequality in society and between peoples are reversed, it will be impossible to eliminate violence. The poor and the poorer peoples are accused of violence, yet without equal opportunities the different forms of aggression and conflict will find a fertile terrain for growth and eventually explode…. This is not the case simply because inequality provokes a violent reaction from those excluded from the system, but because the socioeconomic system is unjust at its root.

This "Apostolic Exhortation" argues clearly that exclusion and inequality are causes of violence, and that the current socio-economic system is itself unjust, and calls for a way of acting globally to ensure that all countries share economic success.

Secular ethics

Ethics has both religious and secular traditions. Secular traditions may struggle to develop the concept of Kant's "categorical imperatives," but nonetheless provide an informed structure for ethical thinking regarding business.

Ethical concepts suffuse not just philosophical writing, but also economics. Adam Smith, who wrote *The Wealth of Nations* and described the "invisible hand" of the market, explained that wealth is "diffused" through society.

According to Nietzsche "The state lies in all language of good and evil; and whatever it says it lies; and whatever it has it stole" (*Also sprach Zarathustra*).

Although of limited use in applied ethics, aesthetics provides a useful comparison as a secular ethical school of thinking without any obvious application to business and organised society. Ethical thinking is not at all confined to traditions of duty, virtue and consequence. G. E. Moore in *Principia Ethica* concludes that ethics is individualistic and proposes that ethical activity includes the contemplation of beautiful objects, an activity which can be (uniquely) known to cause no harm. This view of ethics has little application in ethical analysis of politics or the state, but is a significant philosophical school in itself – Keynes was to describe this as a "secular religion."

Other traditions

Ethics is not the preserve only of Europe and the US. Longstanding written ethical traditions exist in, for example, India, China and Japan, as well as throughout the Islamic world. It is not possible to properly summarise these traditions here (unfortunately). Both Hinduism and Buddhism have atheist as well as religious traditions, which inevitably give rise to highly developed secular ethical thinking. Unsurprisingly these traditions typically do not correlate with European ethical thinking – there is in many cases no direct translation of "ethics": as in other traditions, the idea of a separate way of understanding "right living" does not make sense.

The various schools of Buddhism are derived from a background which is very difficult to relate to modern commerce, but which is applicable to questions about how we live. Milarepa (1052–1135) wrote in a Song of Renunciation that:

> The advisor, meditator & go-between,
> These three persons always cause discord & pain.

His writings and teachings call for the renunciation of karmic acts, which are actions that perpetuate the cycle of existence and suffering.

Nagarjuna (*c.*150–250) denies any ultimate truth, and can be viewed as taking an approach to ethics based on practical decisions and positions ethics clearly within the context of current conventions and thinking.

One of the most influential politicians, teachers and writers historically was Conficius (551–479 BCE): he emphasised the importance of personal experience over following rules, and the importance of knowledge; "what you do not wish for yourself, do not do to others." These teachings are closely related to virtue ethics, and stress the importance of ceremonies (e.g. sacrifice to ancestors); respect for institutions; etiquette (in personal life), in an approach to behaviour summarised as *Li*.

Substance not form

Business leaders and investors are often at the sharp end of decision making, and can have a well-informed perspective on how to run a business ethically, and how to behave ethically in business, even while lacking in some of the detailed understanding of the language and history of moral philosophy.

Modern business leaders as well as philosophers have also made a contribution to ethical debate: Warren Buffett, in a public memo to the Berkshire Hathaway managers (26 July 2010), states:

> We *must* continue to measure every act against not only what is legal but also what we would be happy to have written about on the front page of a national newspaper in an article written by an unfriendly but intelligent reporter. Culture, more than rule books, determines how an organization behaves. (Berkshire Hathaway Letter to Shareholders 2010)

It is worth noting that public discussion of ethics is not necessarily an indication of ethical behaviour or of success. Enron, the failed energy giant and innovator, had a 64-page *code of ethics*, with "foundational values" of respect, integrity, communication and excellence.

A framework for ethical decision making

In *Ethics in Investment Banking*, Edmund Newell and I set out a practical way of thinking ethically by considering the following questions:

1. What values are relevant in the situation, and what bearing will they have in making a decision?
2. What rights are relevant in the situation, and what bearing will they have in making a decision?
3. Who are the stakeholders, and what duties are they owed?
4. What are the likely intended or unintended consequences of taking a decision?
5. What virtues will be developed or compromised by acting in a particular way?

Asking the same questions may not give the same answer, even when faced with similar situations, as ethical decisions can vary based on details of the context and the ethical principles of the decision maker.

Reconciling freedom and justice

In order for a company to understand the ethical issues it faces, it needs to ask a series of questions. It also needs to have a framework to understand the issues raised in answering these questions which will prioritise identified rights and duties, and identify which of those are "categorical imperatives" (inviolable).

Understanding the requirements of shareholders: shareholder interest is typically taken as relating to long term shareholder value. The problem for Boards of quoted companies is that shares can be actively traded, and there is no requirement on shareholders (or expectation) to have to indicate reliably their hold-period in any company. A Board therefore needs to take into account what would be in the interests of a wide group of investors, and unless there are a small number of very significant shareholders, second-guess what is in their interest, rather than being able to simply ask what would be a preferred course of action.

Most institutional investors require freedom to trade in shares, even if only in small quantities. For example, a life insurance company needs to be able to invest money used by customers to purchase policies, and to sell securities to fund pay outs against existing policies. For some stock market indices, such as the FTSE100, constituent member of the index will change from time to time, and some investors will be required to change their holdings. Given *insider dealing* rules, many investors would not want to be asked about major strategic changes, as this would restrict freedom to buy and sell shares, and therefore both to manage their investment risk, and to be able to satisfy demands of their own customers or investors. Consequently, for many investors it is necessary to be able to rely on the management of a company by its Board of directors overseeing its executive.

6
Shareholders and Returns

And do not mix the truth with falsehood or conceal the truth while you know it.

The Qur'an 2:42

Chapter summary

- Shareholders own, provide capital for and derive *returns* in the form of profits and dividends from companies.
- A Good Company is one that is both competent and able to make ethically consistent decisions.
- Investment theory is well understood and generally accepted – it is reasonable that investors apply risk-return analysis to investments, and seek to use capital responsibly and on an informed basis.
- Although there are small-scale successful alternative demonstrations of organising societies without using capitalism, their use and scalability is questionable.
- It is difficult to criticise the ethics of attempts at good stewardship based on rigorous use of investment tools without conflating businesses (which are the investment of an individual or the collective investment of groups of individuals) with the aims and duties of government.
- Individual relationships and business behaviour is built on trust, which is used in a sophisticated way between companies through their use of contractual agreements.

- Some ethical traditions, notably Shariah law, would consider business which is not based on risk-taking to be specifically unethical.
- There is a key contextual question to consider: Can earning profits, or growing profits, be an ethical good or evil in its own right?

Shareholders own, provide capital for, and derive returns in the form of profits and dividends from companies. It is considered economically and financially good practice to consider the risk-weighting of returns and to allocate assets systematically, which is consistent with promoting equality. This provides, at the company level, a discipline to ensure fair and rational investment. It does not necessarily, other than by enabling the development of commerce, further other government policies.

Defining a "Good" company

In *Ethics and Investment Banking*, Ed Newell and I postulated that a "Good" company must be one that is both competent and has proper ethical standards.

In order to be "Good" in the sense of having ethical standards, a company must be able to make informed decisions about how to deliver returns to its shareholders, and how to manage its relations with other groups, including customers, employees, suppliers, local communities and the state. Given its need for a secure political environment and the implications of a poor relationship with the state, appropriateness in managing its tax affairs also has to be considered as part of being a "good" company. A "company" in most contexts refers to a legal entity which has specific protections provided by the state in which it is incorporated, most commonly its liability is strictly limited, and shareholders do not have liability for the company's obligations beyond the level of their investment (in normal circumstances). This limitation of liability is provided and maintained through government and the legal system, and is probably the most obvious basis for the company and its shareholders holding a clear ethical obligation to the government and country in which it operates.

With complex decisions required which affect multiple groups, companies need to make responsible decisions which take into account long-term, as well as short-term, effects.

Companies in some cases are required to report on the wider implications of their activities. This can vary from disclosing carbon emissions, to disclosing tax paid in individual countries in which they conduct business. Transparency across a range of non-financial areas is now considered necessary for a company to be a responsible corporate citizen.

Many consciously ethical investors react negatively to a company not entering into a meaningful dialogue. However, it is unclear whether this is *per se* an overall sign of poor ethical standards, or more simply a sign of poor corporate communication.

Why value and valuation is important

Fiduciary duties of directors are normally associated with having regard to the long-term value of a company, in the interests of all shareholders. Directors in major companies will consider value based on formal methodologies.

There is extensive and commonly understood theory and practice regarding the value of companies and therefore of shares (see "Valuation and cost of capital" below, and for a more detailed explanation see Brealey & Myers *Principle of Corporate Finance*).

As set out above, there is extensive ethical agreement about the importance of equality, even if the precise definition can be debated. In practical terms, for an investor satisfying the requirement to treat individuals equally requires providing equality of opportunity. This will affect the way companies consider new investment to expand capacity, the way institutional investors make investment decisions and it needs to be reflected in an approach to investing which is fair and rigorous.

Investing in securities is now among the more global of activities – international *capital markets* enable governments and companies to raise capital and to expand their businesses cross-border in an unprecedented manner. There is much in this that is not beneficial – some practices in *IPOs* which have been seen in China would not be tolerated in Europe or the US, for example. Indiscriminate and poorly regulated mineral extraction can be dangerous, to employees and affected local communities.

If investment is based on a rigorous process – focused on looking at value using a well understood risk-reward based methodology, then it is not discriminatory in itself, but instead can promote equality of opportunity.

A distinction has to be drawn between a company's core activities – focused on its business activities – and concerns relating to wider social issues. The demarcation between company and government rights and duties will vary depending on the location, the business activity and the context. For example, a company may rely on a government to educate employees, but the company is not normally considered to be in a position where it has the responsibility to educate a population if the government has failed to provide the right education to provide workers for the company.

Valuation and cost of capital

There are a number of methods investors use to value companies. Fundamentally, these relate to assessing the long-term earnings, profit or cash flow of a business. Simple ratios such as a *Price:Earnings* (*P:E*) ratio can be seen to be simplified forms of the much more comprehensive *discounted cash flow* valuation techniques, or *DCF*. The key determinants of value are the rate of growth, the ability to pay dividends and the cost of capital.

Arithmetically, the valuation of a company derived from discounted cash flow valuation is the sum of three component parts: the *net present value* of the cash flows from the business through a defined modelling period (typically of ten years); plus the net present value of future cash flows at the end of the modelling period, derived by either applying a "terminal" value (i.e. the price an acquirer might pay for the company at this time); less the working capital required to fund the business (which is normally but not always a negative number).

The net present value (NPV) is calculated by "discounting" or adjusting cash flows for each year's cost of capital – somewhat similar to adjusting for an interest rate. This has a compounding effect over time, again somewhat similar to applying interest to a loan, (but in the opposite direction of course). This makes the identification of the applicable discount rate or cost of capital one of the most crucial variables in any valuation.

Assessment of the overall balance of risk and opportunity is carried out either explicitly or implicitly in choosing a discount rate. The risk of intervention, such as the change in tax regime, will affect the cost of capital.

The concept of a "cost of capital" is probably universally understood in business, economics and finance. However, it often appears to be either little understood or misunderstood by some politicians, commentators and parts of the media. The Cost of Capital is the return required in order to be able to commit capital to an investment. The higher risk the investment profile, the higher the return required. Debt, which has a more secure return than equity, typically (but not always) requires a lower return on capital.

One typical method of identifying a cost of capital is to take similar stocks, and adjust a market-observed "equity risk premium" for the level of volatility or Beta shown in the trading of similar stocks. This provides a proxy for assessment of risk, even though strictly it may be more an observation on trading characteristics which may reflect risk, but at the same time may not necessarily directly indicate a level of risk. The cost of capital will then be calculated as the equity risk premium multiplied by the Beta, plus the "risk-free rate," taken as the coupon on government securities.

Alternative methods of valuing companies can be undertaken, using assessments based on multiples of balance sheet values or revenue. These have drawbacks – in the case of asset values, these are based on accounting policies, which may not relate to value, and in the case of revenue, revenue is not itself a measure of the value received by shareholders, unlike earnings, cash flow or dividends.

Depending on the maturity of a company's activities (i.e. how high its growth rate is and the level of reinvestment required in the business to maintain its market position), it may make payments to shareholders in the form of dividends. Companies which pay regular dividends can be valued using a Dividend Discount Model, which is very similar to a DCF analysis. Companies in a high growth situation will be unlikely to make dividend payments, and investors will profit through the capital appreciation of the share price, which will reflect growth in earnings. Markets tend to anticipate, rather than rely on just historic data, and so it is the anticipated earnings which is most important, rather than results reported in the past. A company with high growth prospects will therefore pay lower dividends, but if its growth rate is broadly expected to remain high, its value will be higher than a dividend paying company with a similar earnings level. In simple terms, a high growth company should be valued on a higher PE ratio than a low growth company.

Different types of investors may place a different value on dividends – some investors may rely disproportionately on a regular stream of dividends, and therefore value it more highly. The disparity in approach to valuation means that it is not necessarily the case that when one investor sells a share to another, one is losing out or failing to value the share correctly. Cost of capital must, in the end, reflect the return and risk characteristics of investors as well as of the share itself.

Different sectors require different approaches to valuation, although all should fundamentally follow the same basic methodologies. For a mature-growth utility, revenue projections can be straightforward and valuation can be fairly precise (although it can be affected by, for example, political risk – the risk of interference for political reasons in regulatory settlements). At the other end of the growth spectrum, pre-revenue tech companies are difficult to model, given their high but uncertain rate of revenue growth. Valuation of tech stocks can be approached by projecting various (high) compound growth rates in revenue, to give an indication of a range of values, which will be imprecise compared with more mature companies, but have greater valuation upside. Companies in the extractive industries – oil exploration and production, mining and so on – can be very difficult to value and very volatile, as their valuation will depend on the value of the commodities they produce. This can vary with supply and demand over time, which can be affected not just by intrinsic risks – such as geology – but also by extraneous issues such as geopolitical events, and has a high level of inherent unpredictability.

Investors will typically make capital available, provided it receives a return commensurate with the risk of the investment opportunity. Determining the appropriate return on a risk-adjusted basis is essential to ensure that capital is both protected, and that investment is not overpriced.

The methodologies of valuation used by investors – pretty much universally – do not pose obvious ethical problems. They are based on the principle of a company being formed by, funded by and serving the interests of its shareholders. Given that a company benefits from stability, the company has a self-interest and a duty of care in supporting government and society. However, this falls short of an ethical obligation to act as a proxy for government. By extension, some (extreme) views of equality will find ethical problems with the behaviour of companies, from a perspective where companies (and individuals) are seen as existing mainly or solely for the benefit of the state and the wider population. It can be argued that failing to take valuation sufficiently seriously could present an ethical problem, in that it can result in capital being invested in areas where it cannot benefit society, by being usefully applied. This argument must have limitations, as all valuation is intrinsically uncertain, and reducing investment to only relatively low risk companies could harm innovation which would otherwise benefit investors and society.

Despite criticism of "capitalism," there is no successful large-scale alternative model for the investment of capital and application of capital to industry and commerce. In addition, as can be seen in the tech sector, it can encourage and enable innovation. Marxist ideals, which can be appealing in theory, tend to fall down in practice on high levels of corruption and lack of incentives. On a small scale, some communities, including those of a religious persuasion such as the Bruderhof, are able to operate without accumulation of personal wealth, but although impressive these are very much exceptions to normal experience and probably could not be made applicable to most people.

On a very different scale, there are and have been large-scale uses of prison labour which have contributed to economic development. This is something outside the conventional capitalist model, but which economically can provide an alternative. It is currently used on a substantial scale for some types of activity in China.

In countries or societies with rationed capital (i.e. more opportunities to invest capital than there is capital in total), a rigorous approach to capital allocation maximises efficiency and reduce inefficiency.

What is seen as a negative impact of this is a resulting disparity between those who benefit from this system, and those who remain outside it. This does not, however, render the system unethical. Rather, it makes the duty of companies (and shareholders) to have regard to the success of government of especial importance, in order to preserve the system from which companies and shareholders benefit.

Just how long is long term?

Company directors should act to preserve and enhance the value of a company. This revolves around the long-term value, rather than just the value on the next trading day, for example. Defining the time horizon that directors should look at is complicated. There are two different answers to this important question.

Most large companies will carry out sophisticated planning over a variety of different timescales, and focus in particular over a three to five year period. Given the speed of development in world events, and in changes in supply and demand, global commodity prices, new technology and so on, it is difficult to look beyond this with much precision. Oil majors have established over 50 years that commodity price forecasting in almost impossible, even on a scenario basis, and consequently tend to use reasonable "planning assumptions" rather than "forecasts." However, companies are often investing in assets with a 20–30 year life (sometimes longer), and will carry out analysis for individual projects going out this length of time, using a range of scenarios, and will seek to identify and minimise risk over these timescales.

It is also common in looking at risks to consider major risks which could impact in the long term: that is, a risk of an event in ten years' time could affect the value of a company in five years.

For most major companies, reputational risk is part of the consideration. However, the range of issues affecting reputation can often come back to assessing whether something is clearly legal now, whereas in practice perhaps as a result of popular pressure, the law can change over time to reflect popular ethical concerns.

The appropriate view of long-term value is probably, in most cases for a company, beyond the life-span of elected governments (since government terms of office are typically in the four to five year range).

Explaining CAPM (the Capital Asset Pricing Model), its uses and its deficiencies

As a part of deriving a valuation for a company, the appropriate risk-weighted return for a specific assets needs to be assessed, which can be done in various manners, some implicit, some explicit. Perhaps the most frequently used systematic way of assessing this is using the Capital Asset Pricing Model. CAPM takes a cost of capital for a zero (or close to zero) risk asset, adjusts it for the asset class, and then adjusts it further for specific risk. This method has a number of flaws, one of which relies on counter-variance with the market as an indication of risk, another is that the answer provided by CAPM can vary significantly based on the base data-set used in the calculation. Nonetheless CAPM is widely used, not just by investors but also by governments and industry regulators in some form (in assessing the allowable cost of capital for companies and industries). Regulators have used CAPM to assess the reasonable allowed return in many utility and utility-related areas, and it has also been used in considering issues relating to anti-competitive practices.

At its core, CAPM uses essentially the same valuation and risk analysis as the use of relatively simple metrics such as the Price:Earnings ratio commonly used by investors.

Why CAPM is important – asset stewardship, rationing and allocation

We have looked at CAPM, seen that it has practical uses, and that it has major flaws. From an ethical perspective, CAPM is symbolic of the ability to make a reasoned and structured approach to investment and management decisions.

The notion behind CAPM is that it is rational to allocate assets, to understand risk and return characteristics, even if the attempt is imperfect. As a trustee of an investment fund, or as an investor, it is sensible to adopt a coherent and systematic attempt to managing portfolio construction.

A similar approach is taken throughout the chain of investment (at least in theory): fund managers allocate capital, taking decisions on capital allocation between countries, asset classes and sectors. Company Boards of Directors manage that capital to achieve returns commensurate with their business activities, and divisional managers allocate that capital within business divisions to maximise that return.

To what extent does investment theory, and asset rationing and allocation, either support or conflict with ethics? The basic ethical frameworks which have been set out here are virtue-based, duty-based and consequentialist. There is an at least implicit assumption that, in looking at the available universe of investment opportunities, investors will exclude those which are illegal, and are normally likely to also exclude those which would incur a high level of reputational risk (there may of course be exceptions to this). An investor or a company is therefore likely to be implicitly applying some form of ethical screening to the deployment of capital. This screening process could be augmented to include a specific requirement to demonstrate that it is in line with an ethical framework, or actively contradicts such a framework. Companies in general avoid undertaking actions which they believe to be unethical, but the absence of clear frameworks for assessing this makes such deliberations both opaque and potentially ill-informed. Investment proposals typically include analysis of risks and other narrative comments. Intrinsically, such analysis can include ethical issues relating to a variety of factors. As was shown in looking at the *CSR* (or equivalent) reports of major food retailers, a company's identification of ethical issues may be limited if it looks only at a range of identified factors, rather than using an overall framework to identify what questions should be asked: at a minimum, the question can be asked from a duty-based perspective as to who has ethical rights related to an investment, and what the company's ethical duties are to those who would be affected.

Looking at the core concepts within virtue-based, duty-based and consequentialist ethics, there is little which cannot be reconciled with an economic/financial approach to investment decisions and asset allocation.

However, there are some elements of ethical thinking which would be difficult to reconcile with economically based asset allocation, notably issues regarding quality. It is difficult to reconcile aiming to promote equality of outcome (rather than of opportunity) with an approach which accepts the rationing of capital on an economic basis: the idea of CAPM in practice is only to invest to deliver a return at or above the risk-weighted cost of capital for the investment. This approach, applied to executive remuneration would require the minimum paid commensurate with the accepted likelihood of achieving the results targeted. Such an approach does not seem to allow for addressing a requirement to consider equality of outcome as an issue, whereas it can be consistent with allowing for equality of opportunity:

> Utilising a rigorous framework for allocating capital, making investment decisions, and managing businesses/investments can be consistent with principles of Justice – including equality and freedom.

It is however difficult to identify a focus of financial decision making on the promotion of equality, or a specific aim to eradicate inequality. Equality of opportunity, as opposed to outcome, can be ethically implicit in the policies of any company aiming to be as successful as possible. Equality of outcome should, to the extent it is desirable, be properly addressed primarily by governments and not business – companies will be indirectly involved in this through payment of taxes, including any progressive or redistributive policies relating to income taxes. Ultimately, it is not possible to resolve the requirements of commonly understood and accepted investment theory with equality of wealth/income. This indicates as well that attempts to impose simple metrics on remuneration are unlikely to be satisfactory – that is, they will at some stage undermine other requirements on company Boards of Directors.

There will always be elements of randomness, or of luck, in remuneration, especially for executives with remuneration consisting largely of equity. This element – whether luck or chance – can be rationalised in part as relating to the option (highly volatile) value embedded in shares. The move to higher equity-related remuneration will risk intensifying rather than reducing variability and apparent unfairness in executive remuneration:

> *Commonly accepted theories of investment allocation and calculations of risk and return are not compatible with notions of equality of outcome (as opposed to equality of opportunity). Governments may seek to deliver progressive or redistributive taxation policies, to which companies will contribute through taxation, but this will not be a part of a company's expected strategy, or something actively required by an ethical policy. There is a major distinction to be drawn between operating ethically in order to preserve and maximise long-term value, and to go beyond what is ethically required to satisfy popular or political concerns, which are (directly) the proper preserve of government.*

Contracts – trust and law

In moral philosophy and ethics, the institution of a "promise" is extensively studied as the basis for conducting much human interaction. In business, a promise is extended into the greater complexity of a contract. Contracts exist to enable co-operation, for example between companies, on an agreed basis.

Companies are able to operate on a large scale because of the existence and maintenance of a clear understanding of what is understood in a contract. The rule of law is essential to most major companies, and is only able to be provided by government. This places a clear set of ethical obligations on companies – from a *utilitarian* perspective, it is in the interests of companies and government to co-operate to maintain and not undermine stability, for example through the payment of taxes. The reliance of a company on government also creates ethical duties between a company and its shareholders on one side, and government on the other.

Consistency in interpretation of contracts is important in underpinning the effectiveness of contracts, and therefore the ability of companies to operate effectively. As the promises of companies become more complicated, there is a need for greater sophistication to understand their meaning and intent.

Companies operate within a context where they retain discretion in some areas of activity, and may need to give it away in others. For example, a company may give away freedom to decide how much it pays to finance its activities when it issues a "bond" – essentially entering into a binding contract to borrow and repay money, subject to an agreed rate of interest. Conversely, a company will retain discretion on the level of dividend it may pay to shareholders (and some companies pay no dividends). Of course, just as individuals can be considered to cede rights to a government, which then protects remaining rights, so a company is subject to the restrictions of a legislative system. These restrictions also provide the stability required in which to operate. So a company may find that it is restricted by minimum wage legislation, but that government provides a background of social stability.

There are differing approaches to jurisprudence, or how courts interpret the law, in different countries and different legal traditions. Some, such as the US, focus very much on the letter of the law – looking at what exactly is written in legislation and contracts. Others, such as Germany, look relatively more at the "spirit" of the law. Some countries have legal systems which are relatively free of political independence, other countries less so.

Given the differences in law in different countries – legislation, court systems and interpretation of contracts – a company operating internationally must understand how to deal with complexity in how it manages its affairs cross-border. Treatment of employees considered fair in the US would be considered unacceptable in, for example, France.

Companies operate inevitably within the legal context of the countries in which they have operations, and are subject to the prevailing customs and ethical standards of those countries. For a multinational company, this can result in the apparent need to apply varying practices in different markets and businesses. There are attempts, for example by the US, to constrain this through global legislation (such as the Foreign and Corrupt Practices Act), and different countries have different approaches to taxation of extraterritorial profits.

The differing legal systems and approach to ethical issues in legislation shows that there is a difference in the underlying ethical approaches taken: for example, the ethical approach to employment underlying legislation in France varies substantially to that in the US. In the US, freedom of decision making is paramount, whereas in France the state aims to protect the individual and makes greater demands on the company, reducing its freedom. The difference in approach reflects a fundamental difference in the view of the purpose and role of the state, notably in this context in its relationship with companies:

Trust is at the heart of a system of commerce based on contracts. A "good" company should aim to be able to be trusted, regardless of the underlying legal and ethical framework in which it operates. The preservation of the "contract" relies on stable government and an effective legal system, giving rise to ethical duties from company to government.

Islam and financing

Islam has distinct ethical principles relating to finance, although in practice much of Islamic ethics shares a strong link with other Abrahamic traditions, Christianity and Judaism. Islam places a high priority on ethical values in business, notably truthfulness and honesty, and requires openness in contracts. Islamic or Shariah financing is based on risk-sharing – a profit can only be earned if a risk is shared.

Conclusion

The generally recognised processes for assessing equity investment may intrinsically support a number of ethical principles, notably equality. There is no reason why they should be outside the range of normally understood human interaction, and therefore they must be subject to normal ethical consideration. The process of assigning a cost of equity to an investment in, for example, a wind turbine is intrinsically following the same process as a butcher calculating a price for a lamb chop, but with substantially more refinement.

Earning a return on equity is not inconsistent with ethical behaviour, although some philosophies consider it so (e.g. Marxism). Earning an excessive return is unethical, and may be a sign of wider problems (such as anti-competitive markets). Some ethical traditions, such as Islamic law, would consider taking equity risk and earning a return as essential in conducting business ethically.

Surplus wealth will be created in most societal situations – at the most simple level, where there is a good fishing catch, or a good harvest. Using surplus wealth to be productive in turn is reasonable, and can provide more good than wasting it, or leaving it inert in some way (burying gold bars). Investing equity capital – putting it to use – seems consistent with major ethical traditions. The requirement to use surplus capital is a rather literal but nonetheless consistent interpretation of the parable of the talents (Matthew ch 25 vv14–30), and consistent with Shariah law. While the pay of business leaders and sports stars looks high today, calculations of the earnings of Roman charioteer Gaius Appuleius Diocles by Peter Struck of the University of Pennsylvania showed that his earnings of 35,863,120 sesterces in prize money would equate to about $15 billion today.[1]

Is there a limit to how much accumulated wealth can be positive, above which it becomes damaging? As with other ethical questions about finance, ethics is not great at creating consistent and meaningful threshold levels. Too high a return on equity may be damaging (and also self-limiting), but the concept of too much capital is problematic itself, especially with very dispersed ownership of very large companies. That is to say, an individual pensioner in Manchester or Wyoming may effectively own a very, very small holding in Sinopec, a Chinese oil major. This would not make the cash reserves of the investor high, nor would it make the reserves necessarily inappropriate for a company the size of Sinopec. By contrast, a successful entrepreneur or investor, may give a substantial proportion of their personal wealth to philanthropic causes (Bill Gates and Warren Buffett are obvious examples) at a later stage in their career, which will enable a significant positive impact on many, many lives, but will be investing very substantial sums during their career. Provided the previous activity of the entrepreneur or investor was not based on unethical actions, it is difficult to see that the size of the surplus wealth they have under their control is in itself problematic ethically. Conversely, there is an economic answer: very large companies and investors frequently have too much capital to invest to be able to select only the highest return investments, and may be too far removed from new developments to effectively identify them. Consequently, their rate of return and rate of growth will tend to slow. *The ethical question should be about how surplus wealth is accumulated and treated, rather than how much there is.*

7
Employees and Remuneration

Annual income twenty pounds, annual expenditure nineteen six, result happiness. Annual income twenty pounds, annual expenditure twenty pound ought and six, result misery.

Charles Dickens, *David Copperfield*

Chapter summary

- Much of the traditional ethical teaching on remuneration is not based on today's business norms and needs to be applied with careful judgement.
- Many traditions focus on the benefit or desire to allow "free bargaining" to set wages.
- Cicero argued that in making decisions, the expedient or beneficial decision is always the honourable one.
- Proposed limitations on remuneration, notably in the banking sector, are a response to the financial crisis. These may prove to have validity in the short term, but if they remain in place in the longer term risk pushing banking into other jurisdictions with different ethical standards.
- The political basis for limits on remuneration also needs to be considered in the correct context – politicians and political parties have their own incentives, notably to achieve political power.
- Ethics is not well positioned to determine a "right" level for remuneration – the structure and incentives are ethically more important than the precise level of remuneration.

- There are ethical dangers in both systematic excess in remuneration, and seriously under-remunerating employees.
- Thinking around the tenure of an executive is important, but again there is no simple right answer. Encouraging long tenure may encourage risk-averse or autocratic behaviour.
- Many of the character traits which can be the trademark of a successful chief executive can also, in the wrong environment or with the wrong incentives, be destructive.
- Cultural differences will mean that deciding on how to respond ethically in one jurisdiction may result in a different answer to the same question in a different jurisdiction. For example, practice regarding employment agreements is very different between Scandinavia and the US.
- Boards are in place to run companies effectively. This does not require them to act as a substitute for government policy. However, it is wrong to ignore societal concerns. At the least this can be reputationally damaging.
- A bonus can be ethical, but there is an increasing tendency to pay this in equity.
- For most employees, the difference they can make to a large company's share value is so little that being paid in deferred equity rather than deferred cash will rationally make little difference in behaviour. For a CEO it can be a meaningful motivational factor.
- A CEO, if deferred equity can be converted in the event of a change of control, may have an increased incentive to agree to a sale of a company.
- Various groups, notably faith-based investors, have proposed maximum multiples of executive remuneration to either lowest-paid or median-paid employees. Such multiples risk creating perverse incentives (i.e. outsourcing all low-paid jobs), and it is difficult to find any precision behind the numbers used.
- The success of fee arrangements put in place for *hedge funds* and *private equity* create a meaningful point of comparison for company executives.
- Fund managers need to take a vocal interest in the companies in which they hold shares, to hold Boards to account.
- A CEO or management which makes major strategic errors can very easily wipe out substantially greater shareholder value than the size of their remuneration – the overriding criteria for appointment of executives must be their competence.

There is extensive ethical thinking around the subject of remuneration, which goes back to a number of ethical traditions, including the *Abrahamic faiths* and Roman law.

Much of the established thinking and commentary on remuneration needs to be applied with some significant judgement – the context in which, for example, St Augustine was writing is not directly relevant to today's norms, where companies employ many thousands of people (as opposed to the pre-mechanisation norm of small artisan workshops and markets, with even large enterprises often only consisting of 10–15 people).

How far should a Board look at ideas of social justice in setting executive pay? Benedict in *Caritas in Veritate* and Rowan Williams have both argued that commerce is a part of society, and therefore not outside or subject to different ethical rules.

Ethical considerations can be of help in identifying rights and duties, and in assessing how to prioritise different groups. Ultimately, one practical failing of ethics is that it isn't very useful for defining precise numerical thresholds – there is no simple answer to many complex questions over remuneration.

Fair wages

The early Christian Church developed a clear view on settling wage levels. St Jerome and St Augustine both set out the concept of free bargaining to set a just wage, based on Matthew 20:13 "The worker is worthy of his hire." In the Parable of the Workers in the Vineyard, a vineyard owner pays those who have worked all day the same amount as those who start work only in the evening. Augustine held that the vineyard owner had paid the earlier workers what they were owed, and the later workers were paid by gift. Interpretation of parables can vary, and many theologians have not followed the interpretation put on this relating to the moral requirement for wages to be set by free bargaining.

Augustine reflects earlier thinking on a number of issues, including the Roman statesman Cicero (106–43 BCE). Cicero had advocated an approach to ethics based on Stoic philosophy, believing in a natural law based on reason, and using both virtue ethics and *duty-based ethics*. Notably, Cicero argued that there was a duty to the state, including to take part in politics. To Cicero, the honourable choice is also always the expedient or beneficial one. Cicero's *On Duties* was a foundation for much subsequent thinking on political duties and ethics. The implication of Cicero's conclusion that the honourable choice is always the expedient one, is that if this is not the case, then the situation hasn't been properly understood.

Niccolo Machiavelli (1469–1527), author of *Il Principe* (The Prince), took an approach similar to consequentialism, arguing that a leader should have regard to the impact of his actions, but that a wise leader should always aim to be viewed as morally trustworthy.

The question of how to approach executive remuneration depends to a significant extent on whether it is accepted that an executive can deliver consistently top-level results. There are very different views on whether a manager can deliver superior *returns* over time. Psychologist Daniel Kahneman in *Thinking Fast and Slow*[1] compares the track record of an investment *adviser* or CEO with belief in a "hot hand" (a player can hit a "hot" period) in basketball. Kahneman asks "How many successful acquisitions should be needed...to believe that the CEO has extraordinary flair for such deals?" and concludes that "if you follow your intuition, you will more often than not err by misclassifying a random event as systematic" (*Thinking Fast and Slow*, p. 117). Conversely, the long-term track record of some investors seems to provide evidence of long-term systemic outperformance in investment; for example, David Tepper of Appaloosa (who has achieved returns over a 20 year period averaging around 40 per cent), and is implicitly (at least) accepted by investors in major hedge funds, as well as retail investors who follow major investment managers. The level of belief in sustainable outperformance, and the ability of an executive to out-outperform, will make a considerable difference to the level of remuneration a Board is prepared to pay, and a shareholder to support.

Recent limitations on remuneration

There is a bifurcation between the pay of different sectors. Prior to the financial crisis, two sectors which enjoyed very high remuneration were the financial sector and the tech sector. A pronounced gap now appears to be developing, with very high market valuations driving remuneration, equity-related rewards and acquisitions within tech. This does not appear in the main to cause significant political or public concern.

By contrast, since the onset of the financial crisis, there have been a number of measures from governments, regulators and other outside agencies, some temporary some permanent, to limit remuneration, notably for bankers whose employers have received government bailouts. These limitations have been focused both on absolute levels of remuneration, and on the form of the remuneration (i.e. equity rather than cash). The EU's Capital Requirements Directive IV (CRD IV) limits bankers' bonuses to 100 per cent of base salary, or 200 per cent of base salary with shareholder consent. This measure is designed to increase the stability of the banking sector. It is not always clear whether measures are designed to genuinely promote financial stability or alternatively act as a form of collective punishment.

Changes in approach to legislating and regulating on remuneration have shown the limitations of both private companies in managing their own affairs if they become an overriding source of political concern, and of governments in trying to limit remuneration.

There is an ongoing court case brought by the UK finance minister (the Chancellor of the Exchequer) at the UK Supreme Court challenging the EU bonus cap, on the basis that by increasing fixed costs it reduces the stability of the banking sector.

Critics contend that EU requirements regarding remuneration and reporting have been strongly influenced by political groupings which are intrinsically critical of business such as the Green Party, albeit this may also give them greater freedom to look critically at business practices.

For banks in receipt of state funding, who benefited from government bailouts, or who were able to survive due to government intervention to provide general market stability, the ethics of bonuses, and of bankers' remuneration in general, is contentious: there is a cogent argument that under these circumstances, banks should not be required to pay bonuses until the overall economy has recovered from the impact of a financial-sector led crisis.

There has been further consideration of the extent to which executives responsible for banks at the time of the financial crisis should be able to retain remuneration earned in the past. In response to a review by a UK parliament select committee, a letter from Governor of the Bank of England Mark Carney to the Treasury Select Committee[2] states that the banking regulator, the Prudential Regulation Authority (the PRA), would shortly start a consultation to include claw-back provisions for bonuses already vested, but that clawing back pension entitlements would likely be problematic under UK (the Pensions Act) and EU law (the Human Rights directive).

The UK government commissioned Professor John Kay to lead a review of UK equity markets to determine whether changes in governance and market arrangements were required. The Kay Review notably made proposals aimed at changing the short-term culture in equity markets and quoted companies, reviewing fiduciary duties and giving shareholders a significantly greater voice in major decisions.[3] The analysis and detail of the Kay review may not have added substantially to the work carried out in 2001 in the Myners Report on institutional investors. Lord Myners, giving evidence in 2013 to the UK Parliament BIS Select Committee gave a detailed critique of the Kay review:

The Professor barely penetrates the carapace. In some places, he is contradictory. He wants less intermediation, and yet he proposes a new intermediation body. The Professor faces both ways on short trading, as Mr Walker exposed in his cross-examination. There is a lack of consistency. In other areas, the Professor simply misunderstands the issues.

Lord Myners raised major concerns over a range of areas including:

- the understand of stock lending;
- a focus on reward, and a lack of focus on risk;
- lack of substantive recommendations on a trading tax, or taxation more widely – "Why a trading culture is promoted by tax exemption?"

Lord Myners also criticised the process for governance on the Boards of quoted companies, describing a "voting outcome that even the North Koreans would be embarrassed by."[4]

In 2013, the Law Commission commenced work on a review of the fiduciary duties of investment intermediaries, as part of the government response to the Kay review. The Law Commission cites Kay's conclusion that the FCA's regulatory rules fall "materially below the standards necessary to establish" trust, confidence and respect, and instead promoted a shift towards fiduciary standards, requiring prudence and loyalty to the customer. The current identification of detailed standards of fiduciary responsibility for investment managers is complex, and based more on judicial decision than legislation.

The Law Commission introductory paper leading into the review highlighted that in "early" cases on fiduciary duties, judges had linked these duties to "the highest and truest principles of morality."[5] The paper appears to view this positively compared with a "box-ticking exercise," but also queries whether it can be "slippery" to confuse legal rules with morality.

Cultural and jurisdictional differences

There is a fundamental difference between the nature of employment practices in Asia, the US and in Europe. In the US, employment is generally "at will," whereas in Europe it is subject to contractual provisions which are in general set down in both legislation and tested in tribunals and courts. One impact of the prevalent approach in Europe is that supposedly "discretionary" bonuses payable after the end of a year can be judged to have been accrued during that year, or a part year, by an external adjudicating body (tribunal or court). This can restrict an employer's ability to manage costs, and can present a significant difference between jurisdictions.

There are widespread differences within Europe in the reaction to tightening *regulation* on pay. In Scandinavia and countries such as the Netherlands, the approach has been broadly welcomed. In the UK, it has met with active corporate and government opposition (although this is by no means an issue with a political consensus).

An article in the *Daily Telegraph* puts the Barclays remuneration situation very bluntly. It quotes Antony Jenkins, Chief Executive of Barclays, explaining the rationale for an increase in bonus payments: "People are less attracted to come to you, both clients and employees... You get into something of a death spiral."[6]

The article states that a reduction in *compensation* in 2012 had resulted in an increase in the departure rate of senior directors at Barclays' US business from 5 per cent to 10 per cent. Jenkins is also quoted in the same article questioning the effectiveness of increasing further the period for deferral of bonuses (beyond three years), "If you say to somebody I am going to give you a bonus but you don't get it for ten years, that person is going to say: 'That is not worth anything to me and so it won't change behaviour at all'."

In a market which is global, where there are opportunities for employees to join other employers – banks, hedge funds, trading companies, sovereign wealth funds – there is a clear difficulty in effectively capping remuneration. This is in theory possible, but at the cost of reducing profitability and therefore returns to shareholders (e.g. pension funds), and reducing the attraction of banks to their customers. It is difficult at this stage to see the ethical argument for such caps – it can be argued that these are necessary for social cohesion, but this seems at the same time to be transferring major political and social problems to corporations for only a short-term gain, with the concomitant creation of additional social problems (greater unemployment, reduced pensions). If social cohesion were in reality such a problem, moves to cap earnings would cover more than a small number of sectors and be applied, for example, to sports stars.

The level of debate between politicians, including finding the same entity (such as the European Commission) on different sides of different aspects of the same debate shows the complexity of the issues being debated. There is not one specific approach to remuneration in the banking sector which is strictly ethical. Nor are the issues of concern all associated with ethics: many of the problems of the financial crisis also relate to competence. In addition, in any industrial sector it is axiomatic that companies may fail – this can be a result of competition, obsolescence and a number of other contributing factors.

The crucial ethical issue is to have regard to both direct and indirect consequences of decisions regarding the *distribution* of profits – the debate between different schools of ethics can bring a number of red-herrings to bear. A more constructive approach may be to adopt the holistic Buddhist concept of right-mindedness. The theory of justice put forward by Rawls, and Cicero's concept of making the "honourable decision" both accord with this. It is only possible, however, in the context where ethical rules are set out, and a prioritisation put in place.

EU regulation

There has been a difference in approach between countries regarding governance and financial reporting for a considerable period of time. The US implemented major reforms to corporate governance in the wake of the demise of Enron, notably the Sarbanes-Oxley regulations, which put very clear obligations on Board members to take responsibility for company activities and statements.

The EU did not put in place equivalent obligations to this, but in the light of the financial crisis has taken significant steps to change regulation of the banking industry, and also of other aspects of company behaviour across all sectors. The plenary of the European Parliament on 15 April 2014 adopted a wide ranging EU directive on non-financial reporting, requiring the reporting of several non-financial issues by large companies based in the EU.[7] In announcing the directive, EU Commissioner Michel Barnier said that "Companies that already publish information on their financial and non-financial performances take a longer term perspective in their decision-making. They often have lower financing costs, attract and retain talented employees, and ultimately are more successful."[8] This measure affects large companies incorporated in the EU, where a "large company" is a company with more than 500 employees, balance sheet total of €20 million or turnover of €40 million. The Impact Assessment for this measure considered the benefits of information relating to "at least" environmental, social and employee-related matters, respect of human rights, anti-corruption and bribery, and referred to other matters including increased Board diversity.

However, interestingly it has not explicitly considered the question of whether ethics have a role to play in decision making: there remains a focus on reporting, rather than on the framework for decision making. The directive appears therefore to be essentially Consequentialist in nature, whereas from a broader perspective, the way in which ethical issues are considered may be at least as important as consequences and outputs.

The Directive makes clear that to the EU, the role of "civil society organisations" and local communities is important in considering the non-financial impact and activities of companies. This is, at least implicitly, an important consideration in how companies consider ethical and *CSR* issues: there is a presumption of a requirement to report not only to regulators and shareholders, but to a much wider group, whose definition may vary over time.

As set out above, the EU has imposed a limit on bonus payments of 100 per cent of salary, or 200 per cent if agreed to by a shareholder vote under CRD IV, which is designed to reduce incentives for "excessive risk taking" and improve the stability of the banking sector.

The measures passed by the European Parliament require that if bonus levels exceed 100 per cent of salary, then a quarter of the entire bonus is required to be deferred for a minimum five year period. Banks are also required to disclose revenue, tax, profit and subsidy received country by country. At the same time this measure was announced, the EU announced an increase to eight per cent in the minimum required Tier-1 capital.

The only EU member state to vote against this measure was the UK, home to Europe's largest financial sector. However, it has a number of other consequences: for a considerable time banks have sought to reduce their risk by adopting a "low-base, high-bonus" structure. Although this has been undermined by increasing legislation restricting employers' discretion on bonuses, it nonetheless reduces banks' fixed costs. A number of EU-based banks have adopted measures to increase remuneration without breaching this rule, including HSBC which has paid significant "allowances" to bankers. Some banks have made "role-based payments" which fall outside the definition of bonuses. Barclays, for example, disclosed in its 2013 Remuneration Report that "consistent with developing market practice, our approach to CRD IV remuneration *compliance* for the small number of impacted employees is a new class of fixed pay called RBP which has the flexibility to be decreased as well as increased." Neither "allowances" nor "role-based payments" are common forms of remuneration in the UK, or in the banking sector. These payments have been put in place to obviate the measures in CRD IV.

Consequently, two of the results of the EU's actions are that (i) banks increase base salaries, thereby increasing their fixed cost based and therefore their risk of failure, and (ii) banks adopt non-transparent approaches to remuneration in order to obviate the impact of the bonus cap.

Quoted in the *Guardian* newspaper, MEP Philippe Lamberts, of the Belgian Green Party, wished the EU to take the UK to court for allowing banks to circumvent the bonus cap. Mr Lamberts, who was involved in the development of the bonus cap proposals stated: "People like David Cameron and George Osborne are part of the same club. These are people who are really out of touch with reality. They are part of the same class, so I think it is natural for them to defend their interests."[9] This reference to class is perhaps surprising in relation to the question of the stability of the banking sector, which is in the main made up of quoted and state-controlled companies. Class struggle is part of the language of Marx and Engels, and less commonly seen in the 21st century than it was in the mid-20th century.

For a company affected by this type of regulation, there is a complex decision as to how to respond, given that EU headquartered organisations are competing against companies in global markets (not just the EU), with fundamentally different approaches to remuneration.

Novartis and the Swiss referendum

Shareholder opposition to remuneration proposals has been seen across a number of sectors and a number of countries: Novartis' proposals for a SFr72 million ($78 million) retirement package for its Chairman triggered a referendum in Switzerland; Warren Buffett publicly discussed abstaining on the remuneration vote at Coca Cola, where Berkshire Hathaway is the largest shareholder, and unusual levels of institutions voted against remuneration proposals at Barclays, AstraZeneca and Reed Elsevier in the UK. It is important to note that, taking these votes at face value, these companies all enjoyed support by a clear majority of their shareholders.

Switzerland held a referendum in March 2013 in which 68 per cent of voters supported proposals putting constraints on executive remuneration, including allowing shareholders to veto salaries, and banning sign-on and departure payments. In addition, pension funds would be obliged to participate in shareholder votes. Switzerland held a referendum in November 2013 in which voters rejected a proposal to cap executive pay at 12x the pay of the lowest paid, with 65 per cent of voters rejecting the proposal. The result of the combined referendums is instructive: Switzerland effectively voted for transparency, and against rewards for failure. Equally, an attempt to put a cap (albeit a modest one) on multiples of pay failed, by the same majority that passed the first vote.

Comparing Lloyds and RBS

It is interesting to note the UK Treasury's different approach to bonus payments in 2014 at two major banks in which it has a substantial interest: the Boards of both Lloyds and RBS recommended paying the maximum bonuses allowed under EU rules, 200 per cent of base salary. The UK Government, via a body called UKFI, rejected this proposal at

RBS, while accepting it at Lloyds. The difference between the two situations is the progress made towards full privatisation in the Lloyds case, and the ongoing problems at RBS. This places the RBS Board in a potentially difficult position, as given EU bonus caps this means that certain categories of bankers may earn half the bonus level at RBS that they might at competing institutions. Given that the career path for bankers can be opaque, this is a trade-off that many will not accept – the impact may well be for RBS to lose some of its more talented staff. Having said this, it is also difficult at a time when the public sector is urging pay restraint to allow employees at a single state-controlled institution to be paid out of line with other groups of employees.

Is there a "right" level?

There are strong reasons to question whether some of the very high levels of remuneration are in fact necessary, although the question needs to be asked for both individuals and institutions.

In 2009, Jeroen van der Veer, outgoing CEO of Royal Dutch Shell, famously declared:

> *If I had been paid 50% more, I would not have done it better. If I had been paid 50% less, then I would not have done it worse.*

From the perspective of justice, can a compensation package based on external benchmarks and approved by shareholders, which is effective in producing excellent performance, still be unethical? If the compensation concerned is effective, and therefore in the interest of other groups, it is difficult to see an argument that would render it unjust simply on the basis of being high, unless it resulted in the deterioration of the position of another group.

Although ethics should accept the importance of popular concerns, this should not override all other ethical considerations (there are risks of responding to public concerns where this could be punitive or tokenism).

How much is too much?

There must be some realistic limit on how much it is necessary to remunerate an executive. However, when remuneration is based on shares, which may increase for reasons outside an executive's control, it is (i) difficult to cap this, and (ii) sometimes difficult to understand how much of a rise in share price is due to the individual, and how much due to the market.

Rather than postulating a numerical level as the answer to the question of what is too high, it may be more useful to propose considering at what level remuneration is not supported by shareholders, or at which it damages shareholders or other groups.

This (damage to shareholders) can include creating strong public and/or political antipathy to the company concerned. In a related manner, damage could be inflicted on society more widely if a remuneration package (or, more likely, a pattern of remuneration packages) resulted in a risk of losing customers, or a noticeable and actively increased level of popular concern. It should be acknowledged that remuneration packages at wildly different levels can figure on the front pages of newspapers, and consequently this is an imprecise basis for consideration.

How much is too little?

Another way of answering the question of what level of remuneration would be excessive is to ask what would the impact be of systematically underpaying an executive?

The level of remuneration is driven by the needs of appointing and retaining executives in a competitive market for executives:

- The field of possible candidates may be narrowed to exclude those with a track record.
- This may result in the company increasing its risk by looking for relatively untested candidates, or alternatively limiting the field of candidates to include those proven internally.
- Overall, this can increase the risk of a company underperforming.
- A good executive will become a target for other companies, once a track record is established. As a result, a company will be more likely to retain mediocre management for a sustained period.

The right structure, not the right level

Paying a chief executive is not a question of hitting the precisely correct sum. It does not, realistically, matter what an executive is paid within a fairly wide band. For a CEO, the impact that it is possible for one person to make on a company is very significant. It is a cliché to discuss "aligning interests with shareholders," and as has been discussed in the context of, for example, Lehman this may not always work, but this is still perhaps a reasonable description of the intent of executive remuneration.

Objections to high levels of remuneration are probably greatest as "rewards for failure," where a departing executive receives significant compensation, where their departure is the result of unacceptably poor performance.

If it is accepted that executive remuneration, especially that of CEOs, is systematically at a level which is not justifiable, the question becomes one of how remuneration can be reduced. The answer has to lie with shareholders, who own the companies and (literally) appoint Boards of Directors.

Being an executive of a quoted company is not the same as being an entrepreneur, or working within a private equity context. This is not intrinsically because it has to require different skills (arguments that executives are simply not cut out to be entrepreneurs are difficult to prove, and will vary in accuracy in individual circumstance). Many entrepreneurs would not have the administrative skills to manage large quoted companies (or the patience to deal with their shareholder registers). The reason for the difference is partly because of the duties towards a wide group of shareholders, and also partly associated with a normally open-ended period with regard to stewardship of a quoted company – a private equity investor is seeking to acquire, manage and *exit* investments over a defined period, for which the management company is remunerated by its investors. Through owning equity (shares) over long time periods, executives should have the opportunity to earn the highest levels of remuneration, as this will give the highest level of alignment with shareholders. This will not work in every case.

Tenure

The tenure of executive appointments, which in part may relate to the form of payment (largely cash) may contribute to disincentivising long-term commitment and therefore long-term decision making.

It is interesting to look at a comparison between normal practice in investment banks and *private equity funds*: private equity funds tend to pay out to fund partners only when a fund is fully realised (i.e. all assets sold), although private equity funds tend to pay higher base salaries than investment banks. Investment banks tend to pay bonuses annually. Both sectors draw on people who are highly paid with a similar skillset and background (there is a substantial level of progression from *investment banking* to private equity, although less in reverse). The different in the nature of remuneration does not seem to deter quality candidates from working in private equity, and from being successful. The structure of private equity incentivised remuneration actively works to retain employees, especially at a senior level, for relatively long tenures.

Short-term equity incentives, including the conventional structure of deferred equity vesting in the event of a change of control, lead to an incentive for executives to be prepared to "recommend" the sale of control of a business. Conversely, it is notoriously harder to make an approach to acquire a quoted company where a CEO or Chairman is newly appointed, and want the opportunity to play with their "new toys." Although all directors of a company are bound by fiduciary duties, an alternative approach is not unheard of. One UK CEO of a quoted company telephoned a company rumoured to be interested in acquiring the business he ran and said bluntly: "It will be a cold day in hell before you acquire us."

Ego and self-importance

Critics of high levels of remuneration have a valid point when they contend that many executives would take on roles without such high levels of remuneration. In addition to money, many executives have a high sense of personal importance or ego. This can be two-edged: it can cut across duties to shareholders, or it can drive success. Many of the traits which can give rise to success can also be potentially damaging. The role of incentivised remuneration is to encourage directors to act in line with shareholders' own interests.

Increasing the deferral period for equity-related remuneration will help to focus attention on longer term issues. However, many equity-related remuneration structures provide for the equity to "vest" (be released) if there is a change in control. A move to remuneration structures with very long-term (five years +) deferral provisions might result in more executives seeking to orchestrate a sale at relatively modest acquisition premia, which would ultimately be against the interests of shareholders. The problem with incentives, at least a large part of the time, is that they work.

Alternatively, for the more mediocre managers, the incentive will be to worry less about the equity value, and settle in for a long and comfortable tenure without really attempting the difficult work which could seriously improve value, but might be especially taxing or stressful.

Sense of responsibility

People who are appointed to senior positions in companies are dissimilar. They may share certain attributes – leadership, for example – but will have different mind sets. Some will be very intellectual and financially focused, some very operationally detailed, some very strategic. Equally, they will bring with them (and develop) different levels of social awareness and broad social conscience as part of their personal baggage.

If social equality and harmony is the overriding ethical concern, then it is difficult to reconcile at all the typical structure of quoted companies and market-based pay, which was the point very effectively made by the Occupy movement.

Taking the view that the ethical prerogative for a company and its Board is not social equality, and therefore that achieving remuneration fairly in a way approved by shareholders is reasonable, it is important for executives to think broadly about the impact they can have personally, not by using their role for personal profile (which is not uncommon), but by taking an informed interest in broad social issues. This may or may not include philanthropy – many dedicated executives may not feel they have the time to dedicate to such activities prior to retiring from an executive role.

Market benchmarks

There is extensive debate over the need, or not, to preserve value (and competence) by paying what can alternatively be seen as "market rates" or "excessive remuneration" to Board members and investment banks. The dichotomy between the two views can be simply irreconcilable on first analysis: on one view, it is a failure of a Board's duty if it should lose profitable business areas through inadequate remuneration. On the other, it is fundamentally unjust to remunerate executives above certain thresholds or multiples, and by doing so to create social inequality and even civil unrest, which can damage the society in which a company operates. This fundamental difference of views is typical of the issues faced in analysing the ethics of company behaviour to "stakeholders," and in part reflects different ethical traditions – the ethics of rights and freedom, versus the ethics of justice and equality (although justice can be adopted as an argument by both sides of this debate). Attempts to reconcile this difference are problematic. Alternative approaches at resolution can be found in part by appealing to traditions of political ethics, and also by looking at broader concepts, such as the Buddhist idea of *Dharma*. There is much moral philosophy – Cicero, Kant, Rawls – which argues that ethical principles need to be adopted and then set in a hierarchy if "beneficial" decisions are to be made.

2+20 fee structures

One reason for increasing remuneration in publicly quoted companies has been the comparison with the earnings/wealth creation of people paid by hedge funds and private equity funds, where "2+20" fee structures and carried interest or promote based incentivisation has given rise to extremely high rewards.

The fee structures prevalent within hedge funds and private equity funds have enabled fund managers in some cases to accumulate very significant personal wealth, based on successful management of investments.

Fund managers receive a fee of two per cent of investments under management, plus a 20 per cent share in the "upside" or increase in funds. It is common for hedge fund managers to reinvest very high levels of their fees in their own funds.

Some very successful hedge fund managers have increased their fee levels above the 2+20 level, as a way of rationing the quantity of investments they manage, as there are practical limits of scale for some investment strategies, for example of liquidity.

It is important to note that highly sophisticated and wealthy investors agree to pay successful managers of investment funds highly incentivised fees, which can in turn make those investment managers very wealthy. The level of understanding behind agreement to pay such fees suggests that this can be entirely rational economically, even if the fees paid appear immense, whereas this would not be the case if the investors did not fully understand the arrangements.

The managers of the funds pay dues to the state in the form of taxes, which in many countries are "progressive," that is do not relate only to the services consumed by the individuals concerned. In this sense, the fund managers concerned are actively supporting society – provided they pay tax on their income and gains.

The level of fee paid to fund managers appears to be significantly less frequently criticised than the remuneration of executives in publicly quoted companies. The reasons behind this difference could include:

- Publicly available data on quoted companies.
- An acceptance that the skill of fund managers warrants very high levels of remuneration.
- The incentivised nature of the remuneration – typically, the very high levels are based on performance.

However, this runs counter to limitations put in place in banks, where regulators in a number of jurisdictions (notably the EU) have limited bonuses to a multiple of one or two times based salaries, depending on whether there has been a shareholder vote. Fundamentally, the politically driven measures to protect society from mismanaged banks may be in fact broader: they suggest that there is something wrong with levels of bonus a multiple of base salary.

Where the activities of a bank employee may be very similar to those of an employee of a hedge fund (and this may include administrative as well as professional staff), why should there be a difference? This would be merited by the risk of systemic financial failure caused by a bank collapse rather than the collapse of, say, a hedge fund. However, the failure of LTCM threatened a systemic collapse, and the failure of one of the major hedge funds could also have a systemic impact on the financial markets. The response to this could be complex: this could be interpreted as suggesting that hedge fund activities and remuneration should be more tightly regulated, or it could be interpreted as suggesting that the regulation of banks is at least partly politically motivated, and relates to issues other than the pure protection of society from the impact of banking failures.

The argument often presented for "low basic, high bonus," has been that this structure de-risked banks. In the event of a period (a year) of poor performance, the bank was not committed to high fixed remuneration costs. It is also possible that one unintended consequence of the application of changing employment law practices, notably within the EU, has been to make payment of a bonus more contractually fixed than previously, obviating the benefit of the low-basic structure.

Points of comparison

The comparison can relatively easily be made between company executives and those at an equivalent level in professions (law, accountancy) or executives in unquoted companies (e.g. owned by private equity funds), as discussed above.

There are other points of comparison which should be considered when considering the responsibilities of executives. Senior politicians may have significant administrative responsibilities, typically earning relatively modest levels, but also with the potential to earn (in a few cases) very high levels after leaving government offices.

Also, senior figures in the military and in NGOs may have very significant and complex executive roles. The relative lack of rewards has not historically prevented the recruitment and development of high calibre leaders in military forces in a wide range of countries. Many major NGOs are now very international, with very extensive budgets and complex operations. Faith groups also attract committed but (in some cases remarkably) low-paid leaders. The relatively modest level of remuneration seen in these sectors has not prevented some high calibre leaders and administrators emerging.

Does incentivisation work? Can it lead to abuses and asynchronous risk?

The risk-reward trade-off for many highly paid employees is asynchronous: the size of the opportunity very significantly outweighs the risk. This is highlighted by the apocryphal concept of an "Acapulco Trade": this Wall Street idea is that a trader would place a very big and risky trade, then leave for Acapulco, only returning if the trade is successful. The downside, of losing his job, would be limited compared to the upside.

The incentives for highly paid employees can be different from those on Boards of companies and to employees who have significant shareholdings in their employers.

The popular response to high pay and wealth can appear confused. There is a celebration of fame and celebrity, including of wealth, at the same time as excoriation of "unjustified" wealth.

Executives in the public sector, on modest pay, can also abuse their pay and position. Abuse is not the preserve of either quoted companies or the highly paid.

Ratios

Some investment funds – notably some funds associated with ethical and Church Investors – have advocated policies aimed at restricting the pay of a CEO or senior executives to a specific multiple of average or lowest-paid employees. This is philosophically incompatible with the idea of free bargaining in general and the concept of highly incentivised structures –the 2+20 structure in particular.

Higginson and Clough[10] argue that it would be "difficult to justify" a ratio of greater than 75x the average pay of the lowest paid 10 per cent in a company. They also argue that over time the ratio "should be on a downward trajectory." The recommendations in this report, although published by the Church Investors Group, have not been widely adopted, including by Church Investors. The rationale for the approach of using such multiples is normally clearly reasoned. However, the choice of multiple seems (almost) always to be highly arbitrary.

The use of this approach can also create a variety of perverse incentives: for example, a CEO could increase their potential income through outsourcing low-paid work, for example office cleaning, to lower paid agency staff. Alternatively, this might be a disincentive to invest in developing markets where prevailing rates of pay are lower than, for example, Europe.

It is likely that some politicians and ethical investors will return to discussion of the possible multiple-based approach to executive remuneration. This would be a sign that, although the approach has deficiencies, other attempts to remedy the worst excesses of executive remuneration have failed, despite the extensive reforms to reporting and voting arrangements. Although it is difficult to see the approach being free of significant problems, it may have greater validity if other approaches clearly fail.

Transparency

Moves to increase the level of transparency, and increase the power of shareholder voting, may significantly reduce the ethical risk inherent in executive compensation.

The length and technicality in the remuneration reports of large companies may make them impenetrable to small investors. However, typically around 90 per cent of shares are held by institutions, which are capable of understanding the reports. While transparency and openness sometimes seem sacrificed in favour of technical compliance with applicable codes of practice and accountancy, the publication of detailed reports is welcome. The lack of transparency of the workings of remuneration committees can be less so, given the ethical concerns over the sharing of value between shareholders and executives.

Many remuneration committees rely extensively on specialist remuneration consultants, and remuneration surveys. In practice, the higher paid executives benefit from strong equity performance. In addition, executive remuneration may be influenced by comparison with the remuneration received by other comparable groups, such as by fund managers, who may benefit from carried interest or similar arrangements.

Fund managers

The role, attitude and experience of fund managers is crucial to understanding the behaviour of major quoted companies:

> *In researching this book, one fund manager with over 20 years experience privately described executive remuneration as "a conspiracy against the shareholder."*

CEOs have too great an incentive to sell a business, especially toward the end of their tenure. Fund managers can be much less focused on short-term performance than executives, whose remuneration may be linked to share price or measures incorporating the share price, such as total shareholder return (TSR).

The perspective of corporate brokers, who advise companies on their activity in the markets, would corroborate this: CEOs and Finance Directors typically require some form of explanation for even relatively modest movements in share price (of perhaps one to two per cent), which can be in the normal range of trading driven by, for example, programme trades (i.e. not connected to a company's performance).

From a fund manager's perspective, the average length a manager invests in a company is longer than the average tenure of a CEO of a major company.

There are codes of conduct which are used by and apply to fund managers. The FRC (Financial Reporting Council) publishes the UK Stewardship Code, which applies to many institutional investors (those who choose to sign up to it). This Code sets out "principles and guidelines," but not prescriptive set of rules.[11] The Code recommends a pragmatic "comply or explain" approach, although many investors themselves react negatively to companies who choose to "explain" rather than "comply." Notably, none of the seven principles in the UK Stewardship Code makes a reference to ethics.

There is a clear and substantive role for non-executives in representing shareholders and setting remuneration. Neil Woodford, a high profile and highly regarded fund manager, giving evidence to the BIS Select Committee indicated a clear reliance on non-executive directors. However, the skills, time and attitude of non-execs may not be right in all cases – non-execs are not generally "turbulent priests" but are more likely to be relatively pliable (strong executives who are thought to be "trouble makers" are typically avoided by appointment committees). Many fund managers, and commentators, are critical of the closeness of Boards, through relatively high levels of common membership of bodies.

Fund managers are frequently asked by trustees how they charge fees, but are not frequently asked about personal remuneration. It is unclear whether this reflects reticence by trustees, or a focus on the cost to their funds of investment management.

Corporate governance codes

There are a number of codes relating to corporate governance. The UK Corporate Governance Code (formerly known as the Combined Code) published by the Financial Reporting Council (the FRC) addresses a number of issues relating to executive remuneration. While the provisions of the Code are based on the concept of "comply or explain," in the main it includes a number of areas which would agree with the views on ethical requirements set out here, including:

- Remuneration levels should be necessary, not excessive.
- Paying for poor performance should be avoided, and provisions for claw-back are suggested in the event of misconduct.
- A Board, including relevant non-executive directors, should meet major shareholders.
- A Board should publish a remuneration report.

Unsurprisingly, the Code does not set out in detail how remuneration should be set, nor propose any limits. At the outset, the Code states that "corporate governance is about what the board of a company does and how it sets the values of the company." There are some areas which appear crucial from an ethical perspective but are not covered by the Code: although the Code starts out by talking about the Board's role in setting a company's values, little guidance is given on how values should be derived and applied, although the Code is careful to advocate avoiding a "boiler plate" approach. In addition, the importance of ethical values and good governance being part of a decision-making process throughout a company is not acknowledged.

The UK Corporate Governance Code is a significant improvement on earlier attempts at codifying corporate governance requirements. It is succinct, and in most cases very clear. However, from an ethical perspective it still lacks critical depth in key areas – corporate governance has not always accepted the importance of ethics or "values," and in this case while there is much on reporting and voting, there is little on ethics and values. Just as reviews of the financial crisis started by focusing on structural reform, and only as an afterthought acknowledged the importance of behavioural and ethical standards, corporate governance codes still take surprisingly little account of the depth of relevant thinking in the main ethical approaches to behaviour and decision making, and in particular the question of where in the company ethics or values should reside – within the Board or a Board committee, or throughout every level of a company.

Most, if not all, major quoted UK companies (i.e. those in the FTSE100) make a serious attempt to comply with this Code. This does not prevent in some cases very high levels of shareholder dissatisfaction.

Remuneration reports

The Boards of quoted companies produce remuneration reports to set out proposed remuneration for Board members (and in some cases other key employees), and to show how this relates to business performance.

The UK government amended in 2013 the requirements for remuneration reports,[12] which are now required to include:

- information about the remuneration of the directors in the financial year being reported on;
- payments made to directors for loss of office;
- a performance graph which sets out the total shareholder return;
- the percentage change in the remuneration of the *chief executive officer*;
- the relative importance of spend on pay;
- a statement of how the directors' remuneration policy of the company will be implemented in the financial year following the relevant financial year;
- a statement of the result of the voting on remuneration at the last general meeting of the company;
- the future directors' remuneration policy and a future remuneration policy table,
- an illustration of the application of that policy to the directors;
- the policy on payment for loss of office; and
- a statement regarding consideration of the company's overall pay policy and the views of shareholders in the formulation of the policy.

These regulations brought in a number of changes: publishing a single figure for the total remuneration of each director (which institutional shareholders tended to calculate, but may have been complex for some retail shareholders), but more significantly a binding shareholder vote on remuneration proposals.

To date, the reports from major companies have generally been focused on direct issues of remuneration, and tend not to have indicated in detail how decisions are made in balancing the interests of employees (including directors) against other groups (notably shareholders), nor have they generally mentioned ethical issues. Although some reports show that remuneration committees take into account issues of justice and corporate reputation, feedback from remuneration committees and company Chairmen is that such issues are considered in depth, although not within the context of a clear and published framework.

Barclays, which suffered a shareholder revolt over its executive remuneration in 2013, publishes an increasingly detailed remuneration report. The remuneration report for 2012 showed that performance was assessed against a series of targets, and measured against: return on equity, reduction in the cost income ratio, management of the core capital ratio, and an improvement in the dividend pay out ratio. This latter measure clearly takes into account the equity between executives and shareholders.

The major concern of shareholders was a comparison of the bonus pool with dividends: the remuneration report for 2013 showed an increase in the bonus pool (notably for investment banking), compared with a flat dividend.

Barclays, has developed a "Balanced Scorecard" to measure performance against defined metrics relating to Customer & Client, Colleague, Citizenship, Conduct and Company. This scorecard sets out targets for each area, but interestingly not a hierarchy or prioritisation of issues. The presumption is that the company will not compromise in any area, but as the shareholder vote on remuneration shows, this is perhaps idealistic. Ethical policies, in order to be meaningful, must be practical. This does not, however, guarantee universal acceptance or agreement.

Barclays' corporate governance report states: "We endeavour to demonstrate ethical leadership and promote the Company's collective vision of the Company's purpose, values, culture and behaviours. We were acutely aware of public sentiment and of the challenge of presenting shareholders with an increased pool in a year where profits have fallen ... our lack of pay competitiveness was beginning to cause demonstrable damage to our business, especially outside the UK."

Barclays has also sought to obviate some of the impact of EU limits on bonuses (CRD IV), in part because the directive affects EU-based institutions globally, and they are faced with competing against companies outside the EU with greater flexibility in remuneration. For example, US financial services firms (for companies head quartered outside the EU, the EU bonus limits only apply to their EU operations and not to their non-EU operations).

Barclays' remuneration committee stated that it sought to ensure that the balance between shareholder returns and remuneration is appropriate, clear and supports long-term shareholder interests.

However, achieving this in practice is not straightforward. In June 2008 Barclays acquired a "clean" part of the North American business of Lehman. To some extent, operational issues in Barclays in North America may represent problems resulting from integrating this acquisition. In a presentation to investors in 2013, Tom King, Barclay's Chief Executive of Corporate and Investment Banking indicated that 80 per cent of Barclays' Managing Directors in the Americas came from Lehman Brothers. Since 2008, Barclays has undergone very significant management and strategy changes.

Barclays' governance report for 2013 is a complex, sophisticated document. Board membership of major quoted companies is no longer an honorific role, especially in the financial sector. The bank's remuneration and governance committees and its Board have clearly taken major steps to provide a transparent and responsible approach to managing remuneration. At the same time, the result is clearly divisive for investors.

The concern over the implementation of the company's 2013 remuneration proposals related to a wide bonus pool, not just to executive remuneration. Barclays rationale for its level of bonus pool related in a large part to concerns over departures of a group of senior employees ("Managing Directors") in the Americas, who had largely joined Barclays as part of an earlier acquisition, of the Americas business of Lehmans. The remuneration report did not say, but it appears to follow, that the problems which formed the proximate cause of the shareholder revolt related to problems with integrating cultures following an acquisition – a common problem with major acquisitions. The departures would prove particularly costly had Barclays been contemplating a sale of that business, or a spin-off of Barclays Capital, its investment banking business.

As was demonstrated in the financial crisis, where in some cases executives at banks and investment banks suffered huge personal losses, attempts to align interests of executives and shareholders are no guarantee that shareholders' interests will in fact be furthered, nor that the interests of executives will be furthered. Lehman CEO Richard Fuld saw the value of his shareholding collapse from c. $900 million at its peak to virtually zero in a period of just a few weeks.

It is possible that measures to increase the proportion of equity in high remuneration packages will result in an increase in remuneration for some executives, due to increases in share prices pending the vesting period of shares.

Is there a negotiation?

The concern of many institutional shareholders is that too frequently remuneration committees are focused on agreeing a package which satisfies the executives, and at the same time are too distant from shareholders to fully understand their concerns. This would appear to be demonstrated by the surprise of members of remuneration committees at the size of shareholder votes against remuneration, at a wide range of companies (e.g. Barclays, eBay, Novartis, AstraZeneca).

As a shareholder, remuneration committees can often be felt to be too focused on their own processes, and not flexible enough to take into account shareholder concerns, with the result that it appears that there is a necessary lack of one party to a two-sided negotiation. Meetings with shareholders should not be a process of explaining and justifying, at the expense of consulting and genuinely considering concerns.

Can a CEO make a difference?

Recruitment of a successful CEO with a track record of achieving or exceeding their targets (whether revenue, profits, returns or strategic change) is inevitably competitive. An internally promoted CEO who is rewarded with a package above their previous level, but below other companies, will be vulnerable to being poached by another company. The skills required to be a CEO can typically be transferred between companies and sectors making an international market place for recruitment.

There are many examples of the damage that can be caused to a company by a CEO with poor judgement or leadership ability, resulting in the destruction of shareholder value. One example would be the UK's Marconi (formerly GEC), which went from a cash-rich engineering company to insolvency within a relatively short period. The deterioration in the company's position was largely due to acquisitions (or rather, making major acquisitions using cash rather than equity) – that is, management decision rather than a change in the performance of the company's existing businesses. This change was therefore driven by management decisions, rather than being related primarily to pressures on the existing business. A similar comparison can be made about the scale of problems experienced by RBS, following its acquisition of ABN Amro, and the impact of its executives in leading the company ultimately into disaster for its shareholders.

Conversely, a successful CEO can make decisions which substantially increase the value of an organisation. This can be seen in, for example, entrepreneur led companies, including in the tech sector. The impact of a CEO can also be seen in preserving value in adverse conditions (banks such as HSBC were able to survive the financial crisis without requiring government bailouts).

There is a middle ground in remuneration – competent and satisfactory or slightly unsatisfactory CEOs, who are remunerated against market norms, but whose remuneration may not be entirely justified. In many organisations, it is difficult to understand where performance lies for an individual in the middle ground of performance. Incentivised remuneration, involving bonuses paid against targets, or share-related payments (whether options or actual shares), seeks to avoid this problem. However, in situations where there has been a major change in the operating or competitive environment, Boards face a dilemma: the incentives cease to work, and therefore have to be changed.

The effect of high compensation packages on the state is complex: remuneration is an allowable cost, and therefore reduces corporation tax paid. However, personal tax rates for highly paid executives are typically above corporation tax. As a result, the state would receive more tax in any given year from a high compensation policy. Proponents of an overriding ethical obligation to pay corporation tax may be implicitly arguing an ethical case for high executive compensation.

Contract law often makes it difficult to reduce executive (or other) compensation packages in any meaningful way. Poorly worded contracts can also make it impossible to reduce payouts in the event of an executive's employment being terminated as a result of underperformance:

> *There is an ethical difference between two different situations: first, a high remuneration package being agreed where, despite the size of the package the effect is immaterial on shareholders and the state. Second, where the size of the remuneration package has a direct impact on other stakeholders.*

The constraints of employment law in the EU perhaps contribute to an environment where high remuneration packages have different implications than in the US and many developing markets.

How shareholder interests can be compromised

Shareholder interests can be most compromised not only by high remuneration and a lack of a proper negotiation on their behalf, although this can systematically erode returns, but more severely by major events creating very high or uncapped liabilities. The impact of this can be seen in major events such as environmental problems, and possibly from an erroneous focus on financial performance at the expense of other considerations. Examples of this would include, for example, the RBS acquisition of ABN Amro, but can also include operational rather than strategic shortcomings.

BP suffered a severe accident in the Gulf of Mexico in 2010, and has been required by its shareholders to fundamentally review many aspects of its business. The BP remuneration report for 2013 shows how performance can be assessed against different benchmarks for short-term (i.e. annual bonus) compared with long-term incentives. Criteria for annual performance are essentially based on operational performance, including 30 per cent based on safety, whereas long-term performance is based on criteria including total shareholder return (i.e. dividends plus growth in share price) measured against its peer group (other oil majors).

In his introduction to this report, dated 6 March 2013, the Chairman of the BP remuneration committee states "[W]e seek to reflect shareholders' interests as well as to fairly reward the achievements of our executives, recognizing the contentious nature of top executive pay while ensuring competitiveness for our talented leadership."[13]

In the BP remuneration report for 2009, the year before the Deepwater Horizon accident, Dr DeAnne Julius, Chair of the remuneration committee states, "This overall excellent performance was also reflected in the market, where BP shareholders recorded the highest total shareholder return (TSR) of all the oil majors for the year."[14]

Whilst a comparison of the 2009 and 2012 reports shows some changes (e.g. a move from a 15 per cent to a 30 per cent weighting of safety for bonus payments), it is difficult to see the fundamental approach in 2009 having changed by 2012. The major change which has taken place is the deferral of payment of long-term incentives, which can also be seen in the Barclays report (and notably further changes to deferral periods have been queried by the Barclays CEO):

> *The annual reports and remuneration reports reviewed all accept the principle that executive remuneration must be appropriate in shareholders' interests. Neither report has a discussion of the impact of remuneration on tax, and neither do the full annual reports discuss payment of dividends and remuneration in the context of ethics, tax or a form of social contract (see Tax below).*

As BP's remuneration reports highlight, it is straightforward for companies to accept that executive incentives need to be fair, and to be aligned with shareholders' interests. To put this in context, the BP 2012 remuneration report shows total remuneration of £15.5 million or $25.5 million (using a £:$ conversion rate of 1.5), which can be compared with the financial performance for 2012 (shown in the Group Income Statement) of profit for the year of $11.8 billion, tax of $6.9 billion and dividends of paid of $5.3 billion (shown in the group cash flow statement). The provisions made by BP against the cost of the Deepwater Horizon accident total over £27 billion ($42 billion) to date (May 2014):

> *Management failings and skewed priorities can result in short-term gains for shareholders and executives but long-term losses, if the full*

range of risks and responsibilities faced by a company are not under-
stood and prioritised appropriately. Large international businesses are
too complex to be controlled by groups of non-executive directors, espe-
cially those who are independent and best placed to represent minority
investors.

In the case of BP, much of the reporting by the company, which of
course is ex-post rationalisation, shows an overall approach surprisingly similar pre- and post-crisis – which is an alarming similarity.
Where behaviour has no criminal connotations, generally company
law may protect executives, employees and directors from the implications of poor judgement or injudicious behaviour.

For a sustained period of time, Tokyo Electric Power Company
(TEPCO) was among the largest and most highly regarded companies in Japan. TEPCO owned a number of power stations, including
Fukushima, a nuclear power station outside Tokyo. In March 2011,
Fukushima was hit by a Tsunami caused by a sub-sea earthquake,
and was irreparably damaged. The resulting damage caused a release
of radioactivity. TEPCO was part-nationalised in 2012. TEPCO and
the Japanese government were criticised for lax safety standards,
and a culture which failed to provide transparency on nuclear safety
issues. The total cost of the disaster has been estimated at approximately $100 billion.

It is important to put into context the necessity for companies to be
run fully competently, and the difficulty of finding the right senior
management to do so. This is especially the case given the alternative opportunities open to executives, outside the quoted sector. At
the same time, a distinction must be drawn between companies with
relatively modest demands, and those of great complexity or very
high levels of competition or innovation.

There is an element which is missing from remuneration reports –
an attempt to understand the trade-off between employees and
shareholders. In economic terms, what appears to be missing is the
understanding that in the same way that executives merit remuneration, shareholders also merit returns, which in itself is the fundamental principle of all corporate finance. In ethical terms, the
missing element is a discussion of the equity in making payments
from the perspective of the group which actually remunerates executives – the shareholders. To consider merit (in remuneration) without

acknowledging the need for equity (with shareholders) is to inevitably risk an unethical solution.

Using remuneration to solve wider social problems

It can appear as if politicians would like to either (i) solve social problems through private sector companies, or (ii) distract attention from social problems by blaming them on failings of private sector companies (or a combination of the above).

Efforts to solve societal problems through management of remuneration policies could become counter-productive, unless equality of resources (as opposed to opportunities) and redistribution are ends in themselves.

Unjustified high levels of remuneration will create high levels of resentment and therefore public concern. High levels of remuneration need to be justified by performance, and the company's duty to the state and society requires that remuneration should be explained, and not just to equity shareholders (this will apply equally to media and sports stars).

The use and reliance of Boards on specialist remuneration consultants inevitably varies. Some Boards have reported concerns about the approach of consultants, which is criticised for "always pushing up remuneration levels, never down." In the end, it is Boards that are required to use their judgement to preserve and enhance value for shareholders. In the words of one Chairman, "We would need to be deaf and blind" not to pick up on popular concerns.

Social repercussions

There are strong ethical arguments regarding the duty to have regard to society generally, rather than individual self-interest, or the self-interest of groups of individuals (such as for the shareholder base of a company).

A company has a number of shareholders, and for a major multinational company those individual shareholders will come from a wide range of countries. Their interests in the shares of a company will be a sub-set of each of their financial interests.

Shareholders should act responsibly and ethically, and in other respects than their financial interests should also act responsibly – for example to their local communities. There are ethical obligations on individuals, both acting as shareholders and in other aspects of their lives. The ethical obligations on companies are not by any means the major form of obligation on shareholders, directors and employees. There is a significant ethical obligation on executives to be aware of and respond to pressures on society and on local communities where they can make an impact. It is possible for their interest and commitment to be relatively modest during their working careers, but at the same time it is important that they show a regard to wider issues while they are the beneficiaries of high remuneration, part of which results from wider social stability.

A company must be able to understand its own business activities, and should be in a position to act responsibly in its business dealing. This includes having regard for the society in which it operates, which in any case is to its own benefit. However, in all normal circumstances, a company cannot be expected to be in a position to make and/or implement elements of government social policy which are not within its area of activity.

The purpose of government is to act in the interest of its citizens, providing services required by those citizens. It is government that is able, through levying taxes and putting in place service provision, to provide support beyond the level of individual citizens or companies. The type and levels of services will depend on the type of government in a country and can, as observed above, vary significantly.

This relationship between company and government/society will, of course, breakdown if the company does not honour its ethical obligations by contributing to taxes in the jurisdictions in which it operates.

As well as the direct impact of corporation tax paid by a company, the company has other impacts on society. This is notably through how it manages relations with employees, customers and suppliers, which will directly affect many times the number of people affected by executive remuneration issues. The amount paid to executives can have implications: for example, it can lead to a net increase in tax receipts (which in the case of corporate taxes we have argued is a good), albeit this is likely to be marginal. If the amount paid to an executive – no matter how high – leads to higher payments to all other groups, this can nonetheless lead to some ethical problems, even if it may produce ethical benefits. This can be in the form of concern over inequality, or the impact of inequality, and is likely to tie in with ongoing political and popular sentiment, where this occurs. In determining the level of remuneration, a company should consider the risk of adverse impact on society, although the direct impact is likely to be less relevant than the impact on the company's reputation. It is notable that opponents of inequality, who advance arguments from the perspective of "relative poverty" (see below), do not advocate the remedy of executives spending a proportion of their earnings in the relevant local community, which would have the impact of spreading their income and therefore potentially reducing the inequality.

Poverty

Poverty can be defined in absolute terms (e.g. living on an income of $1 per day) or in relative terms. Relative poverty is typically taken as being in the lowest 25 per cent of income. The argument put forward is that this deprives individuals of opportunities available to those with greater financial resources, even though they may not be in poverty in an absolute sense. The concept of relative poverty is one which is derived from a pursuit of equality, and is also often associated with justice.

There have been many attempts to analyse why executive remuneration is high, and why it may not correlate with investor returns. Mihir Desai, of Harvard Business School, attributes it among other causes to a failure to differentiate between luck and skill, and a false comparison of the capability of executives with leading entrepreneurs. Professor Desai describes the situation as "a giant financial incentive bubble." Desai suggest possible reforms, including Boards and major investors stopping using outside advisers to assess performance and remuneration. However, he may not place a sufficiently high premium on the "insurance" factor of hiring or retaining proven talent, or the opportunity cost for a large company of hiring an underperforming manager.

To apply a framework to remuneration based on ethical principles requires selecting and identifying ethical issues as being imperatives and second order. For example:

- An executive should not be remunerated at a higher level for poor performance than for good performance; or

- Executive remuneration should reward creation of long-term value, rather than taking higher risks for a short-term gain.

Approaches which appear to risk negative consequences and which should be avoided include:

- Multiple-based approaches (i.e. limiting executive or CEO pay to a multiple of average or lowest pay). This can give incentives to either increase costs unnecessarily (against the interests of shareholders), or to contract out low-paid activity, or to not use direct employees in low-wage markets.
- Incentives for short-term performance.
- Seeking to use an individual company's remuneration policy to address essentially political concerns (which is a different point to contributing to wider societal problems).

This type of concept is already embedded in some remuneration reports and company remuneration strategy.

Ethical issues and questions which need to be addressed or asked in determining remuneration should include:

- Securing proper stewardship and leadership for the company.
- Ensuring executives are fairly remunerated.
- Does the remuneration pay out higher levels in the event of success and not of failure?
- Is the remuneration clearly in the interests of shareholders and have shareholder views on remuneration genuinely been taken into account (rather than just collated)?
- Are there identifiable circumstances which would make the remuneration negative for shareholders (e.g. termination payments in the case of poor performance)?
- Are there external factors which would result in the remuneration package damaging the company's reputation, and are these outweighed by the benefits of the package?
- Has the right balance been struck between the demands of the executive and the rights of shareholders, so that the package does not represent an unjustified transfer of capital from shareholder to executive?
- Are there external consequences for the host government of the proposed remuneration – that is, will it have a disproportionate effect on or contribute to social instability?

There will be an inevitable overlap between the ethical framework and conventional aims of remuneration: an ethically good remuneration package is one that will play a part in the executive performing successfully. Having an entirely separate structure for analysis of ethical issues after preparing other aspects of remuneration proposals would be helpful, but is likely to be sub-optimal.

The iterations with tax and shareholder returns should not be forgotten:

- Higher remuneration, in most jurisdictions, will result in increased tax.
- Where remuneration is equity based, this may be less clear cut, due to differences between capital gains and income tax regimes.
- Only very high levels of executive remuneration will make a significant direct impact on shareholder returns, but this does not justify an insouciant attitude to increasing remuneration.

Criticism of the process

Executive remuneration structures are typically complex, designed to align executives' interests with those of shareholders, and are subject to detailed specialist advice and intensive deliberations from Board remuneration committees.

This process is subject to criticism that it consists essentially of other executives taking advice from consultants whose living depends on constantly changing compensation levels and structures, and the process lacks any natural restraining effect. Remuneration Committees in general have been frequently criticised, including by committee members, for contributing to spiralling increases in executive remuneration in a context where shareholder returns do not show the same improvement (or deteriorate). The role of specialist remuneration consultants has come in for especial criticism.

There has been specific concern about "rewards for failure" and the size of retirement packages awarded to executives who have already been (presumably fairly) remunerated for carrying out their roles.

Envy

Are there specifically unethical motivations behind criticism of remuneration? Whilst the premise of this discussion is that executive remuneration can be excessive and therefore unethical, there is a contrasting ethical dimension which should be acknowledged. Part of the media and political opposition to executive remuneration may in itself be unethical: stirring popular resentment based on envy may encourage social division, especially where there are arguments which are (publicly) unacknowledged but which justify high levels of remuneration. Frequent comparisons between executive pay and the remuneration of politicians (i.e. the US President or UK Prime Minister) are rather unhelpful, in that they dramatically understate the proven earnings power of senior politicians once they have left office. Newspapers routinely report relatively high salaries paid to civil servants, teachers and so on as a source of concern, and not just the packages of bankers. At the same time, conversely, there is a significant level of interest in "celebrity" lifestyles and income.

Proponents of redistribution of taxation, and possibly also some forms of progressive taxation, might be criticised for causing insta-bility in society, by focusing on what can be distributed from the relatively wealthy to the greater number of relatively poor, which can lead to envy and suspicion, and a culture of entitlement. This can also be seen to be encouraging a group of individuals to seek to appropriate the wealth of others for little reason, and appears to go against religious rules such as the tenth commandment. This argu-ment can be viewed as limited in terms of applicability, as it does not accept the injustice which has led to the current state of wealth distribution.

Conclusion

Executive remuneration presents practical and operational questions, and can also give rise to ethical dilemmas. Appointing and retaining capable executives is necessary for a company to be successful (at least relative to its peers). In ethical terms, the debate can polarise rapidly with little commonality between arguments based on justice on one side and utilitarianism on the other.

Consideration should be given to the question of whether securing strong financial performance is an ethical good in itself – it is clearly aligned with the fiduciary duties of directors. The ethical rights of shareholders to be able to derive a return must be balanced against other obligations, including taking the requisite care to manage a business with due regard to risks, including with regard to compliance (in a very broad sense) and risk.

What are the rights, duties and consequences with respect to high executive pay? These will vary depending on the ethical framework adopted: for example, an ethical framework which sees "relative" poverty as a major ethical problem will see high levels of executive pay as unethical, whereas one that sees higher tax revenues as desirable in themselves will see higher executive remuneration as ethical.

Arguments for constraint on executive pay are generally derived from justice, or duty-based ethics. Arguments for higher levels of pay normally derive from *utilitarian* logic (with its associated flaws). Proponents of justice as a determinant of executive pay typically do not explain the results that their arguments could have on shareholders, other employees or the state. It is difficult to argue that the highest levels of executive pay should be constrained if they can be demonstrated as benefitting all other groups of stakeholders, unless a purely redistributive ethical framework is adopted, rejecting the concepts of freedom and free bargaining. Proponents of such redistribution would be unlikely to accept the ethical validity of a privately funded company motivated to produce returns for shareholders.

Equally, the utilitarian argument for high executive pay can be unconvincing, in that it may be based on the premise that high pay could produce a superior outcome for shareholders, other employees and the state, without necessary limitations associated with virtue or duty. Where a payment is made as a result of failure, high pay is contraindicated by utilitarian arguments themselves.

What is the role in this area for virtue ethics? Virtue has a part to play in this area which seems generally, albeit not deliberately, to be ignored. Remuneration committees have increased their sophistication dramatically, and increasingly look beyond purely utilitarian arguments (broadly, how much would an executive ideally want) to broader issues, such as what the impact of remuneration is on other groups, how the remuneration of executives motivates other employees, and its role in attracting capital or maintaining secondary markets for shares. The level and way in which executives, notably the CEO, are remunerated can play an important part in attracting new capital to a growing business (e.g. a newly or recently *IPO*'d company seeking to develop new product lines), or one which needs additional finance (e.g. an over-leveraged company undergoing a *restructuring*), as well as in maintaining a strong shareholder register. Under these circumstances, many investors prefer to see a CEO with the opportunity to make significant personal wealth, provided their remuneration is tied to the success of the investment – for example, through share-based incentives such as equity or deferred equity. Defining acceptable approaches to agreeing remuneration – from both sides, company and executive – can assist in reforming cultural norms in this area. Where points of comparison are taken from examples outside the most relevant comparator groups (equivalent executives in similar sectors/geographies), these should not only take other highly paid comparisons, but look at broad areas, to avoid the risk of being seen only to be justifying an answer, rather than properly considering the question.

The identification of an ethical component (or an overlay) to questions of setting executive remuneration lies in three areas: first, identifying (as is currently done) the range of reasonable comparisons for the task performed by an executive (i.e. not simply comparing a CEO with other CEOs); second, it is a duty of companies to minimise the risk of paying for failure, (and it is in any case unethical of an executive to seek to be actively rewarded in the event of failure), and ensuring broad contractual terms will not result in unintended payments; third, once this risk is avoided, what is required is a combination of understanding the impact on other stakeholder groups and allowing informed free bargaining – informed on both sides, and properly represented on both sides. The economic analysis of the situation is integral to a just result – the application of ethics in this context, to understand the impact of the payments considered, cannot ignore the economic issues arising, and therefore a very simple solution such as applying a ratio of average pay is not appropriate in many cases (in part to avoid creating perverse incentives regarding low-paid and unskilled employees).

The difference in legislative approach to different sectors looks problematic and unsustainable. The caps on pay may be politically motivated, and will certainly end up accelerating the move of banking and investment banking to other markets. Specialist ethical investors will tend to support restraint on remuneration, and will be less supportive of the rather artificial structures put in place to subvert them. Political attempts to restrain pay may be motivated, for example, by a desire to rebalance European financial centres against

London, which is very much a political rather than public-spirited motivation. Pushing banking and investment banking expertise from Europe to the US, Middle East and Asia may prove unproductive for the EU, and remove decision making from an environment where ethics are relatively strongly embedded.

8
The State and Tax

Render unto Caesar that which is Caesar's.

Mark 12:17

Chapter summary

- The state raises taxes to fund the services it provides its citizens, in areas such as policing, education and healthcare (although services will vary between countries).
- Individuals (and companies) cannot choose which areas of funding they will cover through tax.
- Ethical arguments can be advanced both to support and to criticise tax avoidance.
- Elements of redistribution (of earnings, as opposed to wealth) can be ethically desirable, and in practical terms beneficial for companies.
- There are some positive reasons for executives to manage tax, including by enhancing earnings by deferring tax, but these can have negative consequence, increasing longer-term risk despite having a NPV benefit.
- Governments sometimes make grandiose claims about the ethical requirement to pay tax – the ethical obligation on companies is in general unarguable. However, in using tax as a form of comparative advantage, government behaviour can significantly undermine the specifics of tax payment. Governments (of all mainstream political persuasions) offer tax breaks, and compete with each other for corporate investment.

- Tax breaks enjoyed by charities, churches and similar groups are allowed by governments, provided they do not undermine overall public sector priorities. Such groups benefiting from tax exemptions do not always recognise the balance of their contribution to society, which includes a shift of the tax burden to income taxes of middle earners.

- There are many anomalies with regard to national and international taxation: the tax status of the United Nations, the use of retrospective taxation, such as "windfall" taxes, which are a tool used by many governments to raise funds. The existence of such devices underlines the pragmatism as opposed to idealism underlying government funding.

- Governments have failed to individually or collectively respond fully to the globalisation of research, manufacturing and marketing. This has profound implications on corporate taxes, has already led to low corporate taxes, and potentially could lead to an end to northern-European models of welfare payments, other than in resource-rich countries.

Taxation funds the activities of a state. There are areas funded by tax which are generally agreed to be part of a state's duties, such as the defence, the legal system and security of its subjects. Other areas which are seen as a public good may also be funded by tax in many countries: childcare, policing, education, healthcare, emergency services. These services provide an environment which enables individuals to fund, grow and operate businesses.

As well as funding services required to support its citizens, a state may raise taxes to carry out activities which are ethically ambivalent, such as overseas military operations.

In general, tax is not hypothecated – tax is collected centrally, and only then distributed by a state's finance ministry. Consequently, it is not possible for a taxpayer (whether a company or an individual) to decide on ethical or other grounds to support some parts of a state's activities and not others.

There are different possible approaches to avoiding paying tax, some of which are clearly illegal and unethical, some of which are legitimate, others more ambiguous. A distinction is drawn between tax "avoidance" and tax "evasion": the former is legitimate, although the ethics of this behaviour are questioned, and the latter is by definition illegal. Within the general area of tax avoidance, terms such as tax "structuring" and "optimisation" have become more current, along with the concept of avoiding "tax leakage." The description of some practices or structures as "aggressive" has been used pejoratively by politicians in describing practices which they see as going against the spirit of tax legislation.

Complex and aggressive tax structuring is not a new phenomenon. US President John F. Kennedy criticised "artificial arrangements between parent and subsidiary regarding intercompany pricing" in a "Special Message to the Congress on Taxation" (20 April 1961).

The standing of tax is in essence straightforward from an ethical perspective: governments are necessary to maintain order and stability and a range of services from which companies benefit, and companies have an ethical duty to support the legitimate actions of governments, including raising taxes to fund these activities.

It is possible to argue both for and against tax structuring on ethical grounds, and the nature of the argument depends both on an analysis of rights and duties, and the nature of the company's tax position. Companies have a duty to shareholders, and a some-times offsetting duty to the state. Tax avoidance from a utilitarian perspective might be supported in some circumstances (resulting in increased investment), and opposed in others (reduced welfare payments). However, an analysis from a number of specific virtue perspectives is more likely to oppose tax structuring, although at the same time it can support increased investment and increased dividend payments (thereby, for example, augmenting pensions). A number of activities carried out by the state, such as healthcare and education, would be consistent with accepted ethical ideas of virtuous behaviour. Actions by a company which reduced tax payments may therefore be considered in some circumstances to be contrary to specific concerns of Virtue ethics. There are limita-tions to how far this argument can be taken, as in most cases a state will be reliant on continuing tax revenue and other benefits such as employment provided by companies, and therefore will need to ensure that companies are able to continue to operate effectively, including with regard to reinvesting in their activities and remuner-ating shareholders for their investment.

From a utilitarian perspective, in the medium to long term it makes little sense to pay no tax, as this undermines the state, and therefore the stable and secure environment in which to conduct business. However, from a short-term perspective, it can be argued that not paying tax could be beneficial, although given the impact if this approach were common, this is not a fully coherent argument. Redistribution (especially of income) can be advanced from a utilitarian perspective, in that it will provide for the greatest overall satisfaction within a population. However, this has certain caveats: it depends on (as exists in many countries) a relatively small number of people being net donors, and a relatively large number of net beneficiaries; it also has limitations around the impact of redistributive policies on incentives to invest and earn, and obey tax laws. A level of redistribution may be beneficial, as it may reduce the risk of civil unrest.

Remuneration, incentives and tax

J. K. Galbraith in *The New Industrial State* argues that the company is not run solely for shareholders. This perspective is important, as companies are the property (collectively) of their shareholders. However, given that companies have an interest in preserving relations with employees and the state, as well as customers, suppliers and local communities, the concept of a company needing to ethically have regard to groups other than shareholders should not be contentious.

There is an iteration between incentive arrangements for executive remuneration and tax. Arrangements which place targets on net income, TSR and so on will encourage tax optimisation. Dividend paying companies tend to maintain stable "dividend cover" – which implies that an increase in net income will lead to increased dividends. Given the relative size of tax bills and executive remuneration, the impact of tax optimisation would not realistically be swallowed up by increases in remuneration. It is worth noting that executive remuneration – including incentive structures – are typically subject to shareholder votes. It would be going too far to say that this suggests that shareholders are mandating executives to minimise (rather than just manage) tax, as remuneration structures are very multifaceted.

Criticism of corporate tax

Tax commentator and reformist Richard Murphy argues that proponents of both zero tax and paying any amount of tax are incorrect.

He contends that ultimate shareholders (as opposed to their *advisers*) do not really argue for tax to be minimised, and that minimising tax is carried out for the benefit of employees at the expense of all other stakeholders.[1]

This argument could essentially be expressed as executives are incentivised to manage short-term net income or earnings per share (EPS), potentially at the expense of long-term value. This however does not take into account real world behaviour by investors, who when acting as shareholders tend to show a higher level of self-interest than Murphy assumes – that is, there are wider sources of pressure to secure short-term performance than executive remuneration. Evidence from investment and fund managers is that trustees are relatively rarely focused on quarterly or short-term performance above all else.

The type of situation Murphy envisages is similar to the risk of a "rogue" trader – an asymmetric risk profile for an executive. Moves to pay increasing proportions of bonuses in deferred equity should counter some of these risks to a significant extent – whether vesting periods are long enough to manage the risk of deferred tax assets is however unclear. Companies deciding to use tax deferrals tend to focus on the (probably unquestionable) NPV benefit of doing so.

Ultimately, the ethics of tax are tied up with the ethics of the specific tax jurisdiction, which normally equates to a nation state or country. Like many other aspects of political ethics, there is only a limited amount about tax which is necessarily an ethical issue. This is demonstrated by the different tax regimes in different jurisdictions (to pay 17 per cent corporation tax is acceptable in Hong Kong, but would be unacceptable in the USA, UK or Germany). Tax authorities each make demands on companies which in some cases can exceed in total the profits of the companies themselves – simply paying the tax that is asked may not be possible, or desirable.

Deferring tax payments can make rational economic sense for a company. If the tax payment remains the same, and the company's cost of capital means that the Present Value of the payment therefore reduces, deferral of tax represents a risk-free investment for a company's shareholders, provided that it does not increase the intrinsic risk of the business, or result in an unjustified transfer of value to another group (such as executives).

It is tenable ethically to test the boundaries of what is acceptable in seeking to negotiate with tax authorities – which in any case is required by major and international companies. There are limits to how far this can be taken:

- structures put in place to circumvent legislation;
- taking advantage of obvious mistakes in legislation;
- materially or systematically increasing business risk to an extent not explained to shareholders;
- distorting reported profits to maximise remuneration.

It is noticeable that these limits are not one of scale, but of intent and effect.

The gulf between pronouncement and legislation

Government policies and resulting legislation, especially regarding tax, may vary from public statements by politicians, both in government and in opposition. Of course, how much of this is deliberate as opposed to shortcomings in drafting is not always clear – although governments have access to substantial specialist resource both internally and in the form of external advisers.

It can be difficult for companies to be expected to second-guess the intended spirit of legislation where this may vary from actual legislation. The difficulty is compounded by the relative rapidity of change in tax law, and a lag in respect of international treatment: for example, changes in corporation tax rates or capital allowances. There is no single "ethical" rate of tax to benchmark for purposes of deciding if a company is a "good company," or single ethical choice of jurisdiction or set of jurisdictions.

Consider the question of whether a UK or US based oil company with operations in the Central African Republic should, if there is any discretion, choose to pay tax in the UK/US or in the CAR. In the first instance, the head office is in a developed country, to which the oil company has an ethical obligation. In the second, although there may be some risk of greater inefficiency in the use of tax proceeds in the CAR, there may be more benefit for a greater number of people from an increase in tax proceeds. No matter which decision the company makes, it can be vulnerable to criticism in the other jurisdiction for not fully fulfilling its duties.

Competition between governments and countries can undermine the notion of tax payment being an ethical requirement.

Tax as a tool for comparative advantage

Individual countries attempt to use (and sometimes publicise their use of) low levels of corporation tax and tax incentives to attract investment, presumably at the expense of other potential investment destinations. This practice undermines some of the more grandiose claims of tax as being part of a simple equation to create or maintain a fair society.

Michael Porter set out the idea of comparative advantage for companies, and then developed the idea further in the Competitive Advantage of Nations.[2] Porter argues that a country's success is related to the strength of both company and workers, and that the key to success is high and rising company productivity.

In a working paper entitled "What Is a Competitive Tax System" (which provides a thorough summary of the issues surrounding international tax competition), Matthew Stephens of the OECD argues for greater international co-operation:

> countries will want to protect their tax bases. They can do this unilaterally to some degree, e.g. by the regime they operate for the passive income of controlled foreign companies, for the deduction of interest and other expenses or for double taxation relief. The effectiveness of such measures would be strengthened if international cooperation is enhanced…. to ensure that taxpayers engaging in aggressive tax planning are no longer able to shift the burden of taxation onto more compliant taxpayers through other (distortive) taxes having to be higher than otherwise.[3]

As a source of comparative advantage, taxation has the advantage of transparency, but the disadvantage that it is easy to copy – where one country offers tax incentives and low rates of tax, others can follow (at least in theory, there may be complicating financial and political issues to consider). Low corporate tax rates can be seen as improving the efficiency of capital invested in businesses, and therefore contributing to a competitive environment in which business can operate.

Corporation taxes are not the only area of tax which relate to competitiveness – income taxes, social security costs and so on all also affect the overall competitive environment of a country. In addition, the effectiveness of ensuring that (illegal) tax evasion is identified and penalised will have an impact on the competitive position and therefore success of companies.

Much of the international approach to tax co-operation was based on agreements reached in the 1920s, to avoid double taxation reducing investment. Double taxation remains a concern for many mature asset-intensive industries, but is not so relevant for businesses built on intellectual property which is highly mobile.

To return to the HFT analogy: HFT works on the basis of creating a comparative advantage, but is criticised in part because it does not actively contribute to an increase in economic well-being. If this is considered unethical, so must much of the incentives put in place to attract businesses to invest in specific regions, which by definition must be at the expense of another region.

The UK has followed a policy of having the lowest corporate tax rate in the OECD, reduced to 20 per cent of taxable profits. When similar countries offer differing tax regimes and incentives, there is a clear temptation to see tax as just one part of a country's approach to care for its citizens and institutions, rather than as the overriding source of provision to satisfy those duties. Given employment and consumption taxes, corporation tax is not the single source of revenue derived from investment and commercial activity.

Louise Story, a journalist at the New York Times, has written extensively about competitive tax incentives across boundaries between different US states, and the damage they can cause.[4] According to Story, Shell has been offered a tax credit worth as much as $1.6 billion over 25 years from Pennsylvania, which competed with West Virginia and Ohio for an energy production facility. Story also claims that subsidies and incentives transfer funds from education to business. The complexity of government approaches to investment by business goes beyond taxation, and can be seen in particular in their treatment of, for example, banks and car manufacturers.

The Scottish National Party (SNP) which forms the administration of the Scottish parliament set out its policy on corporation tax ahead of the independence referendum. This demonstrates how corporation tax can be identified as a strategic tool, in the context of a political party/administration with a strong commitment to social welfare: the proposed policy was to reduce tax to 3 per cent lower than the UK rate, presumably to attract or retain investment at the expense of either the remaining UK (more likely), or potential EU partners (also possible). At the same time, this undermines the concept that a certain level of corporation tax is required to support services. By focusing on a discount to a neighbouring country, rather than identifying a fair rate of tax, this may look like an example of a government looking at the prospects for its own citizens, and not at the position for example of the poor in other countries, or at the impact on the non-corporate tax base in Scotland. While tax is used as this type of strategic tool, it is difficult for companies working globally to ignore the incentives it provides.

There are some countries (relatively few) with zero tax for companies or individuals, such as Dubai. These countries typically benefit from substantial natural resources and can fund their activities without levying tax. This phenomenon raises complex issues about both tax and state ownership of assets, as well as the nature of individual countries themselves. Fundamentally, for ethics to be of value when considering global issues, it needs to be able to offer consistency in dealing with both resource-rich and also chronically poor countries, although the implications on behaviour in each situation can be very different: for example, it would be highly unethical to deny children a state funded education in an affluent country, but a chronically poor country may have no resources to do so, and its failure to do so could not therefore simply be considered an ethical failure. An overview of the historic development of modern countries shows clearly that their creation in many cases depended on actions – including invasion and insurrection – which would be considered unethical in a modern context, and in many cases was unethical at the time. Systems of government often ascribe to themselves a level of legitimacy which may go beyond that which can be genuinely justified. As changes in government during 1989 in eastern Europe and the Arab Spring in the Middle East showed, prevailing government can be changed rapidly where not benefitting from popular support (perhaps unless it resorts to extreme oppression). Government therefore has a vested interest in proclaiming its legitimacy, in the same way that the mediaeval church canonised member of ruling families, thereby endorsing their legitimacy – it should be remembered that going back to much earlier traditions in many cases, monarchs are "anointed," that is, their appointment is presumed to be on behalf of God.

Given the extent of international competition for investment, and incentives and alterations to tax regimes, countries may compete in practice for both investment and taxable profits.

The source of some of the supposedly unethical behaviour by companies lies in large part (but not exclusively) with the governments which use tax as a source of strategic advantage. The more aggressive tax planning developed by tax advisors and carried out by companies is also unethical, where it clearly exploits unintended loopholes. However, this is not an adequate summary. It is for example the nature of internet businesses that they can grow (or fail) remarkably rapidly. The development of internet-based business is actively encouraged by many countries (including the US and UK). Part of the basis and mind set of these businesses is to develop new ways of doing business, using "disruptive" marketing and trading strategies. A part of this naturally results in seeking to take advantage of incentives offered to be based in low-tax jurisdictions. Taxation, and government co-operation, has not been able to fully respond to the challenges presented by internet-based global business (look at Bitcoin). It is interesting to compare the ethical acceptability of government seeking to encourage investment by offering tax breaks with companies considered ethically unacceptable for attempting to manage an uncompetitive situation by finding other ways to mimic tax breaks. Companies need to be mindful of the social implications of their activities. It is not clear, however, whether poor ethical practices (other than extreme) actually change consumer behaviour.

Leverage and tax

Companies use leverage, or debt, to improve their efficiency by reducing the average cost of capital employed. Very high levels of leverage, especially involving inter-company loans from related parties, can be an indication of structuring designed to minimise tax payments and obviate tax rules. Such structures may be relatively common in mature industries with strong cash flows.

It is conventionally understood that interest payments, unlike dividends, are a legitimate cost of conducting business, and therefore interest should be deducted from profits before calculating the amount of tax to be paid.

This approach assists in allowing relatively mature companies to either reinvest shareholder returns in new capital assets, or alternatively for cash to be withdrawn (i.e. through dividends) to be invested in other assets, notably in new businesses with a higher growth profile.

Restricting the ability to treat interest costs as tax-deductible would make a significant change to the cost of debt, and therefore to the cost of products and services.

However, there are circumstances where the level of debt utilised within a company can be excessive, and is designed to reduce the tax burden, rather than to optimise the cost of capital. Under these circumstances, many jurisdictions have the capability of disallowing some element of interest payments from tax deductions, but this rarely seems to happen in practice. At the stage when the level of leverage results in a company paying no (or virtually no) taxation, then a part of the debt burden is effectively acting as equity. Typically, this type of structure will exist in circumstances where there is a complex corporate structure, with cash flows, guarantees and debt in separate legal entities (maybe cross-border); or, in companies where there is an over-leverage resulting from a change in business dynamics, and where therefore a restructuring of debt may be necessary at some stage. In the former case, tax authorities need to be able to see through to the intent behind a structure (and intent can be very difficult to prove). In the latter, aggressive action from tax authorities could result in an insolvency, to the detriment of shareholders, creditors and the state. Where the debt includes a significant proportion of inter-company debt, and in particular there is inter-company debt with no default provisions, it is difficult to see this as anything other than equity. Inter-company debt can be used notably where different legal entities in the same structure are registered in different jurisdictions, to manage tax liabilities, as well as to maximise incentives on and for management. In these circumstances, high levels of leverage are relatively likely to be essentially meaningless – that is, they will essentially be equity capital, but reducing tax liabilities.

Progressive taxation

Progressive taxation is designed to reduce income inequality based on the ability to fund payment of tax – that is, it places the tax burden most on the "broadest shoulders," without actively seeking to redistribute wealth in order to create equality or eradicate inequality. It can be argued that the accumulation and preservation of wealth is only possible through a stable political environment. Therefore, it is in the interests of the wealthy to pay proportionately higher levels of tax and support or allow a level of income redistribution, in order to preserve this environment.

Progressive taxation is understood to provide relatively high levels of popular satisfaction (higher than other approaches), and is favoured especially from a consequentialist perspective.

Taxation does not only consist of corporate and personal income taxes. Sales taxes (e.g. VAT, TVA) tax the consumption of goods; local and property taxes pay for local services, but may be levied on a progressive basis. However, determining details of how a progressive taxation systems works can be problematic, if the aim is to ensure that business can operate effectively, at the same time as supporting low-earners and those without an income. There can in practice be a close similarity between a progressive and a redistributive approach to collecting taxes. Issues which affect decisions on how tax rates and thresholds are set to implement a progressive tax policy include how companies and higher rate taxpayers will respond to high or increasing taxation, and how society values income received by the low paid as opposed to high earners. There is a discrepancy between the electorate and the tax base under such a system which can give rise to ongoing tensions, even though it is designed to maximise "utility."

Progressive taxation works quite simply in theory: increasing rates of taxation as income increases, with corporation tax typically around the rates paid for higher rate tax payers (although there is significant variation on this latter point). In practice, collecting tax receipts as thresholds increase and levels of redistribution increase can become less simple to forecast – that is, rates of tax increase but actual receipts can decrease. Former adviser to US President Ronald Reagan, Joel Slemrod, writing about progressive taxation concludes that "upper-income taxpayers responded to sharply lower tax rates by changing the timing of their asset sales and by abandoning financial stratagems such as tax shelters that were attractive only because of the special tax treatment they were given. So marginal tax rates do matter, but perhaps not as much or not in the same way as many economists thought in 1980."[5]

Redistribution

It is a fundamental tenet of some political theories, such as most forms of socialism, that government should seek to use its tax raising powers to actively redistribute wealth from those deemed to have a surplus to those who have relatively little wealth or earnings. This can vary in extent, from relatively high rates of tax levied on high earners, to active tax of accumulated wealth, in order that not just income but accumulated wealth is redistributed.

Redistribution of wealth is a policy which can be justified through both utilitarian and virtue ethics. However, neither argument is free from a significant range of challenges, as both presume that equality is per se an ethical good. This is in contrast to the more generally accepted argument for progressive taxation, which is that it results in greater overall satisfaction, and is necessary to provide a stable and secure society. Although there have been a number of attempts to implement redistributive policies, they have been notably unsuccessful.

In practice, a progressive tax system can share some attributes with redistribution. In a number of scenarios the major difference between a redistributive tax system and a progressive system is likely to be the tax treatment of accumulated wealth and property. Redistribution may have the negative effect of reducing the freedom of an individual to have property rights, as the state is taking part of the property to redistribute it to others.

Flat taxes

A number of countries – notably Hong Kong and Russia use some form of a "flat tax." This works on the basis of setting a relatively moderate single tax rate on all sources of income. The advantage of this – as seen in Russia – is that by markedly reducing the rate of tax and its complexity, the level of tax raised can be increased significantly. In Russia, the tax rate is set at 13 per cent. In Hong Kong, the flat tax rate of 17 per cent is applied to corporate profits. In Saudi Arabia, tax rates vary between national and international workers. The major criticism which can be levelled at a flat tax, is such a system is not "progressive," that is, it has no redistributive qualities at all, and can result in low and middle earners paying higher taxes than under a progressive system, which can reduce the overall satisfaction of the population.

Having experienced a decline in public finances, Slovakia moved from a flat tax to a progressive tax system in 2013. In order to meet a requirement to raise increased tax revenue to support government spending, tax rates were raised on corporate earnings and for high earners. An additional tax was also implemented for some (mainly elected) politicians.

The ethical implications of a flat tax system are significantly different to those in a progressive tax system, notably regarding issues of equality, the provision of services by the state and the overall role of the state. Although the fundamental role of the state will be unchanged (to provide stability, protect its citizens), some of the detailed expectations of duties of a state and the virtues associated with paying tax will be different, especially rights: the state is not consciously aiming to promote social cohesion through taxing those who can pay high tax bills, and therefore its citizens may not be assumed to have the same rights to support from the state as in a progressive system.

Flat taxes tend to be favoured and proposed in two circumstances: they have been implemented by countries such as Russia with a history of widespread problems with collecting taxes. They also tend to be (predictably) popular with relatively affluent groups, who see them as a fairer way of paying for public services.

Having regard to the ethics of taxation

As a generalisation, the provision of stable government for the good of the people governed is an ethical good, (although clearly there are questions over the definition of stability and who the governed may be, which can have more than one answer).

It is therefore both a matter of self-interest and an ethical good to support the government, including by supporting its activities through taxation, and failing to support this becomes unethical.

The fundamental duties of a state relate to the protection of its citizens. In terms of services provided and the financial treatment of citizens, the stated basis of government raising taxes varies very significantly between different countries, and can also vary between the governments of a country over time. The services provided to citizens can be very different, from a basic level of "protection" by armed forces, to a more paternalist approach providing a very broad range of services: for example, the government of Sweden provides comprehensive health care to all its citizens, whereas the government of the US asks its citizens to mainly rely on private providers and private health insurance.

Companies are typically expected to pay taxes due in whichever state they incur tax liabilities. This raises a series of complex issues regarding the ethics of paying taxes in an individual country, and also of paying in multiple countries where a company has an element of discretion in how its legal structures and tax affairs are managed, or where tax can be an influencing factor in a decision regarding where to invest or to locate activities.

As an example, consider the merits of using an offshore entity as a head office for a division, which will then carry out activities in multiple countries. In practice, there is a proportion of revenue which can be attributed with an element of discretion, thereby affecting its profitability and tax liability in each country.

The fundamental issue here is whether and to what extent company directors should directly consider the support of individual governments to be an ethical requirement on them.

The requirement on companies must be to support the governments of the countries in which they operate, as good corporate citizens. However, this should fall short (in most circumstances) from making political judgements. A company seeking to produce a long-term return for shareholders may find itself disadvantaged if it takes obvious political positions, and it may also risk behaving in a way which undermines government.

Even governments who aggressively argue that taxation is necessary to provide support for their citizens also act in a way to attract international investment, which may be regardless of the impact of their activities on other countries. This type of competition can also occur between regions or states in an individual country.

In the absence of clear international agreement over taxation, it seems difficult to argue that companies should or could be required to have regard to the ethical standing of differing tax rules: according to Ronald Green, different tax systems may by based on different ethical principles, including equity and equality "every decision about who and what should be taxed involves important moral decisions about values like fairness and justice."[6] Green discusses five key values which he has identified as having a bearing on tax policy: freedom; material well-being and employment; health and welfare; equity; and distributive justice. Different countries and governments will prioritise these issues differently.

There is a complex iteration between personal and corporation tax. The taxation of high individual incomes is typically at a higher level than the rate of corporation tax. Consequently, if a company is able to choose how high to set executive remuneration, absent other considerations the tax paid will in total exceed that which would be paid from lower remuneration. As money is transferred from the company to its employees, the related tax paid on this will move from being paid by the corporation (i.e. shareholders), to being paid by individuals (employees), but the state will have larger tax receipts.

The conundrum this presents highlights the importance of looking at the three major stakeholder groups together, rather than considering the merits of payments made to one or two groups only.

Assessing how to treat taxes should involve consideration of the rights and duties owed to and by the company, and principles of equity, distributive justice and freedom.

The presumed moral value of "freedom" is different in various ethical traditions, and has a very significant impact on taxation. There should be a natural tendency for the position of companies to be relatively individualistic, and therefore more focused on freedom as a key ethical principle, as opposed to politicians who may tend to be relatively more collectivist. This key difference in ethical frameworks may explain a major difference in expectation and behaviour. The value placed on the ethical importance of "freedom" also may be higher in countries which have experienced oppression and therefore value freedom of choice having been denied it.

Equality of opportunity, and equality of material possessions are not simply modern concepts. In particular, religious groups have practiced forms of community living for millennia based on common rather than personal ownership. Organisations such as the Bruderhof appear to continue this way of life today, with individuals and families sharing ownership of material possessions within a community. The notion of equality – developed but not exemplified by Engels – forms the basis of redistribution via taxation. Much of the ethical understanding underpinning this view challenges central tenets of capitalism, to an extent which is effectively irreconcilable. Strict equality of wealth can be criticised for being unjust, in that it could imply taking property from individuals regardless of how the property was accumulated, and without regard to the manner in which it will be used by the recipients.

There is a profound implication of an argument for an overriding ethical obligation – to use Kant's phrase, a categorical imperative – to pay corporation tax. The problem is that all companies pay tax, the question is not simply how much effort they go to in order to manage or reduce the tax payments, but rather whether the tax structuring is based on exploiting loopholes, and/or goes clearly against the spirit of the law. It can be difficult to judge the spirit of the law by taking ministerial statements, as these may be addressed at an electorate, and too imprecise (or inaccurate) to help in assessing tax legislation. There is also a difference in the type of discussion that can be carried out meaningfully with different tax authorities, depending on their overall philosophy and approach.

The purposes of levying and collecting tax will be varied – broadly speaking between big state and small state models. However, this difference does not obviate the ethical basis for taxation. Is all tax fair? Given that different countries have very varied tax regimes, it is tempting to say that some tax regimes must be unfair. This is not necessarily the case: tax has an interplay with other aspects of society. Countries with high taxes, such as Norway, can offer widespread social benefits. Low taxation is not the preserve only of liberal economies, and may be equated with poor social structures. Alternatively, low tax rates may reflect a need to attract investment to a very poor country. In each of these models, tax could be "fair" and just, despite the differences between them.

Tax avoidance is intrinsically different from tax evasion in that:

- It does not directly involve lying.
- It follows the letter of (although arguably not the spirit of) the law.
- It is ultimately transparent to the state (or states) concerned.
- However, on the first of these points, tax avoidance may involve deliberately misrepresenting facts, or hiding information.

Governments need to ensure that their tax base remains intact – it is counter-productive to tax excessively, resulting in a reduction in incentives to earn profits (and therefore an ability to pay tax or be taxed), invest capital and an increased risk of capital outflows to more attractive jurisdictions. Attempts to legislate to prevent "capital flight" tend to be less than fully effective. Equally, it is necessary to attract investment, and for that investment to be priced appropriately, or the cost of goods and services will rise.

A proportion of companies will inevitably always aim to argue for better treatment. John Avlon writing in the Telegraph (30 March 2014) observed: "some CEOs privately grouse that they would rather invest their capital in one-party states, not only because of the rate of return, but also because they feel America's political system is increasingly inefficient when it comes to making long-term decisions."[7] The retort "they would say that, wouldn't they" is inviting here, but at the same time there has been a reappraisal of implicit government guarantees and support for some sections of commerce and industry in the light of the bail-out of the financial services industry, combined with record levels of fines paid (frequently by companies which have not admitted wrongdoing). In reality, there is no real sign that the US lacks financing appetite. However, the cost of financing major projects in the US is greater than in western Europe, notably Germany and the UK, where returns on investment in infrastructure are typically *c*.8 per cent compared with 10–14 per cent in the US. In theory, the required return for investment in an individual project is related both to the individual risk-reward of that project, and to the supply-demand relationship of capital looking to make investments. There is a strong argument that the basis for higher returns in the US is that investment capital is more rationed in the US due to its higher economic growth rates than Europe (an alternative explanation would include the concept that either European or US investors systemically mis-price risk).

I have argued that companies have both an economic self-interest in behaving in such a way as to support the governments in the countries in which they operate and an ethical duty to do so. This is not just a one-way relationship. The governments also benefit from providing a stable environment to operate a business and to invest capital: providing an unstable environment for investment results in an increase in costs for government and the population, and also will result in a reduction in available investment. The inability of governments during the financial crisis to simply alter the cost of debt by reducing interest rates – the LIBOR "spread" or premium above base rates rose to *c.*5 per cent for a sustained period – demonstrates the need for governments to work together with commerce and the "markets" in order to provide the stability sought by the general population.

Does tax evasion have any ethical justification?

Accepting that there is an underlying ethical duty to support the state, and that lying is ethically wrong, it follows that tax evasion is unethical.

There are some reasonable arguments which can be developed to justify tax avoidance, even perhaps aggressive tax structuring (i.e. knowingly exploiting loopholes). However, the position of tax evasion, that is, illegally managing to not pay tax, is also worth investigating. There are extreme arguments that all tax is unethical and a form of theft, which are sometimes advanced in favour of non-payment of taxes. Such arguments have little validity in a modern nation state (whether or not a democracy). In other contexts the arguments may have some validity in cases where a regime is genuinely despotic and "evil." However, at such a stage, the moral position of a tax payer is likely to involve some form of resistance (it is not the place here to debate whether the ethical requirement is for passive or active action), and non-payment of tax would probably be only at a mild end of a spectrum ultimately ending in either imprisonment or exile.

This argument could be extended to a "tax strike," aimed at provoking a change in government policy through mass action. Such activities are normally associated with personal or local taxes – such as the widespread non-payment of the UK "poll tax" in 1989–1990 – rather than corporate taxes. In extreme circumstances, it is more normal to see companies divest or close activities – as happened in apartheid South Africa in the 1980s.

Tax evasion by individuals is much more widespread than by companies (whose accounts are, in the main, audited, and who are required to keep records of economic activity). The level of activity in the "black economy" will vary from country to country, and depend also on cultural heritage. It is clear that there is a greater temptation in areas of activity typically centred around cash transactions (taxi-driving, small-scale building, many trades such as plumbing and decorating). Some countries have a greater incidence and acceptance of such practice, such as Italy and parts of southern Europe. Where these incidences are high, there does not necessarily seem to be a correlation with in principal objections to government raising tax. Evasion of tax is tempting in that it can be extremely simple, and therefore the temptation can be strong. However, the ethical implications of tax evasion for an individual will be as great as for a company and the penalties may be greater – including prison in many jurisdictions. The Chicago gangster, Al Capone, was ultimately arrested and imprisoned on tax charges.

Tax evasion may therefore in very limited circumstances have an ethical justification, but one that is unlikely to arise in other than a despotic regime, or as a response to an individual instance of egregiously bad government. The complication here is that the response of withholding tax may undermine a government more generally – and in many cases, this can be a greater ethical harm than the benefit that large-scale evasion of tax would offer. A decision to withhold tax on ethical grounds is therefore very profound, and the stage at which it is undertaken is one at which the evader will be cognisant of the likely penalties.

Tax evasion will almost always be unethical, although it can be justified in very limited circumstances – essentially as a form of protest against an overwhelmingly despotic or unjust government. The ethical implications of evading tax are similar for both personal and corporation taxes.

Charities and tax

Can a tax-exempt status be justified, and where should boundaries be drawn?

The exemptions from tax given to a charity can raise questions over the extent to which taxation is an ethical necessity. Take, for example, a charity which provides small farm animals – perhaps goats – to parts of sub-Saharan Africa. This charity will pay no tax on its income. Ethically, the actions of the charity may be beneficial. However, if the overall purpose of taxation is considered necessary to support a state, the charity may be behaving unethically in paying no tax. Alternatively, the overriding benefits of taxation may be overstated by the governments which levy and collect the tax.

If this latter view is correct, it would support the freedom of company directors to interpret their fiduciary duties as requiring them to manage their tax affairs actively.

If a government viewed charities as carrying out desirable activities, provided that charitable giving was at a finite level of taxation, then it could respond by reducing the tax benefits if tax receipts reduced or charitable giving increased.

If the level of money avoiding the taxation system through charitable donations were to grow unexpectedly for a sustained period, it is entirely possible that the level of tax break would be reduced. It could be argued that this would be to protect the essential activities of the state. In other words, up to a very limited extent charitable giving furthers the aims of the state (even if only because to reduce the tax benefit of charitable gifts would be politically unpopular), but above an undefined level it becomes a burden.

Tax relief on charitable donations does not remain static. Overall it is designed to reflect tax paid, but this can vary. In the UK, on 6 April 2011, the amount of gift aid – tax that charities can claim back from donations by tax payers –was reduced from 28p to 23p in the pound, as "transitional relief" put in place in 2008 expired, and gift aid was reduced to match basic-rate tax rates. Higher rate tax payers remained able to claim the difference between basic-rate tax and higher-rate tax (currently 40 per cent or 45 per cent) on their tax returns.

Various NGOs and charities have criticised companies and individuals which structure their tax affairs in complex manners. However, critics of tax structuring and high remuneration speaking on behalf of organisations or institutions should note that their own institutions inevitably form part of the system they criticise, and may not simply represent informed and impartial observers. It should be noted that there may be an inconsistency in criticising organisations for both reducing their tax payments and for paying high levels of remuneration, in that remuneration attracts higher rates of tax (for high earners) than corporate profits.

Tax benefits offered to charities offer no strong unethical connotations for donors. However, charities themselves need to be careful to understand that their tax status may be essentially a matter of political convenience for governments, and in practice may undermine the activities of government. The tax position of tax-exempt charities can be complex – their tax status can in some cases undermine the provision of services which they themselves support. This may be an issue easily resolved by charities, but at the same time places them in a slightly ambiguous position, and makes their own views on corporate tax and personal remuneration less unbiased and impartial than sometimes seems to be claimed.

The United Nations

The rather Alice in Wonderland world of tax ethics takes on further complexity when the position of international institutions such as the United Nations (UN) is considered. The UN and similar organisations (the World Bank, the International Monetary Fund) do not pay tax, and the UN's employees do not pay tax, although they may be taxed on UN earnings in their home countries. For US citizens employed in the US by the UN, the situation is more complex: the UN reimburses tax payments, but US citizens are obliged to complete self-employment tax returns to the US tax authorities, and to pay half the cost of their social security (or more accurately, they pay the full cost and the UN reimburses 50 per cent of this). This can be rationalised on the basis of saving international governments money on funding necessary international work. However, employees of NGOs pay tax on earnings, as do government servants, including those involved in parallel activities to the UN – such as peace negotiations.

The logic of the UN not paying tax, and its employees being exempted from tax, is convincing – it saves substantial cost and complex administration. However, at the same time it undermines some of the more fundamental arguments over the ethical nature of tax (and therefore the ethical obligations of and to the modern state).

The EU

Chapter 4 of the European Union Treaty[8] deals with cross-border tax in articles 63–66. Article 63 states that all restrictions on both "payments" and "movement of capital" between member states of the EU are prohibited. Article 65 allows member states to take measures against those who infringe national tax laws, without prejudice to Article 63. This appears to both compel member states to allow cross-border trade, and to allow them to prevent infringement of tax rules, provided this is "without prejudice" to the free movement of payments and capital.

The complexity of this is shown in the European Court of Justice decision on a VAT (sales tax) fraud case brought by HMRC, the UK tax authorities, against Teleos, a company dealing cross-border within the EU in mobile phones (Case C409/04). The judgement allowed a company to rely on statements made by third parties, provided it is acting in good faith, even when there was underlying fraud (and therefore illegal tax evasion) involved in the trade.

HMRC's guidance in relation to similar situations concludes that tax authorities need to make a "rounded judgment about the reasonableness of the action at the time, and without the benefit of hindsight."[9]

Internet

With much retail and wholesale trade now taking place over the internet, there is no obvious single way for a multinational company to decide where profits should be taken and tax paid. The convention that taxes are based on agreed "transfer pricing" values is workable, but imprecise. In practice, the transfer value of goods or services is subject to a number of different approaches, resulting in a reasonable level of discretion in where profits are booked. Transfer pricing valuations and formal "opinions" are offered by accountancy firms and specialist professional advisers. These can be backed up by extensive data and analysis. However, in practice valuation cannot be entirely precise.

Although some companies argue that they obey all relevant tax laws, there are areas of tax law which clearly are rapidly outdated by changing trading patterns. Consequently, there is both scope for tax arbitrage by moving operations across borders, and in addition technical obedience to prevailing tax rules may at the same time appear a (flagrant) abuse.

The role of the internet in society has evolved as a phenomenon, not planned, which changes daily lives in unexpected ways. It is unsurprising that governments have struggled to deal with its impact on business.

The impact of the internet, as seen in the case of social media, may not be what its proponents always set out to claim. For example, Alice

Marwick, a researcher focused on this area, writing in the New Scientist magazine (10 May 2014) on "social media's broken promise" looked at practices associated with the digital economy, and observed that "I knew that while technology companies often paid lip service to egalitarian principles in public, their primary concern was not 'changing the world' but profit … Silicon Valley is famously unequal."[10]

According to Marwick "Rather than encouraging openness, transparency or authenticity – let alone activism or freedom – social media has re-inscribed a limited view of success and a surprisingly narrow range of acceptable behaviour."

There will undoubtedly be further changes in the relationship of government with companies which conduct most of their business over the internet. Concerns over whether there is a level playing field, and about maintaining personal freedoms, often conflict, and are not easily resolved. They will have to be addressed, and readdressed from a tax perspective, and the pace of change in tax law nationally and internationally will itself need to change, if tax systems are to remain fair (as they typically claim to be) and in particular, international approaches to tax co-ordination will also need to change in pace.

Developments to global trade and investment have moved at a staggering rate. Government response, while not being glacial, has not been rapid. And international co-operation has been slow, and undermined by individual countries' efforts to use tax as a source of comparative advantage. This does not make decisions simple for international companies seeking to deliver a return to shareholders while behaving responsibly regarding tax, and creates tremendous opportunities for those companies seeking to behave irresponsibly.

Windfall taxes and policy changes

Working on a transaction for a FTSE-100 listed UK company a few years ago, involving the issue of an innovative form of equity derivative, the company required detailed tax advice. When its legal and accounting advisers returned from consulting "leading counsel" on the matter, the head of tax at one of London's leading accounting firms opened his comments by saying "Everything we have told you about tax over the past 10 years has been wrong." While this may have contained some level of hyperbole, it is clear that companies genuinely struggle to understand the "contract" between them and government. This can result in unexpected and sometimes punitive changes in tax regime. For example, at times a "windfall" tax has been levied across whole industries.

Levying a windfall tax is a political risk for a government, and presumably only carried out if it there is a high level of confidence that it will be both fiscally and electorally beneficial. However, the ability of governments to behave in this way undermines the argument for companies to treat tax in a completely transparent way – governments will normally have too many conflicting priorities to be able to be completely high-minded when dealing with individual companies or industries.

Equally, the incongruity of some tax exemptions raise questions about the nature of taxation: why should internationally acclaimed athletes receive tax breaks to compete in major competitions, which are not shared, for example, by employees of charities, and when in some cases these athletes are already relatively wealthy? The answer relates, of course, in looking at the greater good – intriguingly, if this is viewed as an example of virtue, it could be argued that more tax breaks should be offered – that is, it could be argued that it is good for government to stimulate the economy or national pride by offering tax relief on an individual's earnings.

The windfall tax levied against UK power companies in 1997 raised an estimated c.£5 billion to fund the New Deal (an employment programme), and was a cost to mainly international acquirors of privatised UK companies (many of the shareholders were US companies). A previous windfall tax in the 1980s was raised against the UK banks, when they had benefitted from government policy aimed at reducing inflation – a very high interest rate compared with inflation, gave unusual levels of real return.

There does not seem to be any significant evidence that these taxes caused long-term harm to the sectors concerned, or to customers, although they must have significantly adversely affected shareholder returns for a period. It is interesting to note that one instance was applied to a price-regulated sector (electricity distribution), and one applied to a sector which was not price-regulated.

Questions raised by lotteries and gambling

There are distinct ethical questions on tax and public finance which help to illustrate some of the wider problems with tax compliance and putting in place an ethical framework to consider issues relating to taxation.

Lotteries resemble to some extent a form of regressive taxation: they tend to take money from the less well-off and redistribute it to causes favoured by the more affluent: in the UK, the lottery has supported opera companies and renovation of rural churches, for example. Why are lottery winners not taxed, and not criticised for not paying tax? Is it because they have the same opportunity we have (provided we pay for a ticket), in which case why argue for wealth to be redistributed based on need? Most rigorous ethical frameworks raise questions about unearned income – there is an incongruity between allowing lotteries, but criticising underserved pay outs to executives, and taxing inheritance (which has already been taxed). An exemption from taxing gambling can be justified based on the idea that it is immoral to profit from gambling. This makes a state-supported gambling operation an interesting subject for ethical debate: a leading Church of England Bishop described the National Lottery as an example of "regressive taxation."

Before 1 September 2007, in the UK gambling debts were not enforceable. Under the Gambling Act 2005, gambling debts became enforceable thereafter (the National Lottery was brought in under separate earlier legislation). With the enforceability of gambling debts, gambling losses then became able to be treated as deductions from taxable income under certain circumstances. This treatment makes not taxing gambling earnings appear inconsistent, especially from an ethical perspective: that is, it is obviously inconsistent to allow gambling losses as a deduction, and not to tax winnings, at the same time as arguing that corporate tax avoidance is unethical.

The difference between tax treatment of gambling winnings can be very different between countries, and this difference can cause additional problems. Winnings at poker are taxable by the IRS in the US, but not by HMRC in the UK. As a result, a UK citizen who is a "non-resident alien" in the US will pay 30 per cent of winnings in a withholding tax in the US, but will be unable to reclaim it in the UK, as double taxation treaties between the UK and US do not apply in this area, as the UK does not tax gambling winnings. In the US, there has been litigation involving the IRS on the question of how poker winnings are treated, notably on the issue of whether, if winnings are taxed, losses can be applied to offset winnings (or other earnings). A District of Columbia appeal court judgement in July

2013 held that non-resident aliens are able to apply losses against winnings from the same gambling *session,* in line with the IRS treatment of US citizens.[11]

A complex governmental attitude to lotteries and government is also reflected in other institutions. The Church of England Ethical Investment Advisory Group advises against investment in companies who have major interests in lotteries and gambling. However, many individual churches accept money from the National Lottery Fund (which distributes lottery proceeds):

> The certain liberalisation of the UK's gambling laws is set to increase the accessibility of gambling activities to the population at large, and is no doubt a future area of growth for the leisure industry. This growth is likely to increase the number of those afflicted by gambling addiction and gambling related problems. This may be exacerbated by the softening of the public perception towards gambling following the success of the National Lottery and the large number of people who participate. This is of concern for the Church. *"EIAG: Gambling and Gaming – Entertainment or Exploitation":*[12]

> A historic church near Corwen can go ahead with plans to repair its spire after learning that Heritage Lottery Fund (HLF) have earmarked £123,000 for its restoration fund. St Beuno's Church in Gwyddelwern has been awarded a first round pass by HLF. This means that providing the plans progress satisfactorily, St Beuno's will be awarded the money in 2015 and will use it to repair the spire and church tower as well as replacing roof tiles and guttering. The church closed in 2010 because falling masonry from the roof had made the building unsafe. It's hoped that repair work will be completed during 2015 allowing St Beuno's Church to reopen for church services and community use.[13]

Conclusions

The question of funding can raise complex ethical questions, which can be capable of more than one answer while using a conscious approach to make ethical decisions. This is the case for many questions of public finance and taxes. It is unlikely that the ethics of gambling changed overnight in 2007, but in the UK relevant legislation changed.

An ethical approach to taxation, and by implication public finance, needs to take account of both (i) legal requirements, and (ii) additional ethical issues, in order to ensure that company behaviour remains intact from changes in standards of scrutiny over time.

Payment of tax should be fair, and governments should ensure that collection is fair. The principal of equality before the law is long established, as Dr Thomas Fuller wrote in 1733 "Be you never so high, the law is above you."

Governments cannot be assumed to all have equal legitimacy. There is no single model of government worldwide: the UK has a constitutional monarchy, the US is a republic and China has a one-party state. In various types of democracy, the strength of a democratic mandate will vary according to how much time has passed since the last elections, and the size of a political majority (or lack of it). In addition, it is clear that sometimes governments – even generally good governments – can pass bad laws, or pass laws for narrow electoral reasons. Tax laws are determined by governments, and given the force of law. It is difficult for companies or individuals to try to interpret the spirit of laws, especially when private explanations frequently differ from those made publicly. The prevailing approach in ethics to tax is summarised by "Render unto Caesar that which is Caesar's." The context of this statement was paying tribute to an occupying power, rather than providing services to a government's citizens, (although it should be acknowledged that some theologians interpret this as a statement about the ritual uncleanliness of an image of Caesar in the temple). This of course is complicated when (i) different governments each claim a share of the same profits, and (ii) tax rules are sufficiently complicated, especially regarding interaction between tax jurisdictions, that there is no single way to calculate tax payments.

Many problems associated with payment of tax relate to the globalisation of business. As Stephen Green observes in "Good Value," globalisation is a "phenomenon" which can't be reversed "to treat it as something that is being steered by anyone, or any group of people or any group of countries, is to misunderstand what is really happening."[14]

An understanding of globalisation is necessary to understand the ethical implications of the business structures put in place by multinational companies. Seeing it as a global phenomenon, as Green states, makes structuring decisions by companies a necessary set of decisions. Given that tax incentives are put in place by governments, it is difficult to see that companies are incorrect to take these into account when making investment decisions. Conversely, structures put in place purely to take advantage of tax "loopholes," where form takes precedence over substance, would represent unethical decisions (but would also be relatively dangerous from a value standpoint). I suspect the middle ground in this area will typically be expansive. Failures of policy makers to offer tax regimes suitable for the trade and investment that they actively garner is not something which should fairly be blamed on companies.

The occasional use of windfall taxes is instructive: it demonstrates that for governments, taxation can be both pragmatic, and also that governments can feel able to rewrite rules on taxation significantly and retrospectively when it suits them. This has two implications: first, it will reduce the credibility of arguments that it is up to companies to interpret the spirit of tax rules; and second, it will highlight in some circumstances the need for government to take action to preserve social stability, in the face of popular and political criticism of corporate earnings and investor returns.

Governments have failed to individually or collectively respond fully to the globalisation of research, manufacturing and marketing. This has profound implications on corporate taxes, and will lead to low corporate taxes, and potentially an end to northern-European models of welfare payments, other than in resource-rich countries.

9

The Rights and Duties of Shareholders, Employees and the State

> *You should always perform your duties with detachment, for a man attains the highest good by performing actions with detachment.*
>
> The Bhagavad Gita

Chapter summary

- Shareholders provide capital to start, run and grow businesses. It is reasonable for shareholders to derive a return from investing/risking their capital.
- Capital requirements vary as a company grows.
- *Returns* that investors achieve can vary over the life of a company. Taking excessive dividends increases the risk of the business, reducing its value.
- Boards have to consider the interests of a company, and aren't well placed on their own to determine the wider needs of society.
- There is no simple calculation as to what level executive remuneration should be set at. Shareholders take the major risk, and should stand to make the major gains if a company is successful. An executive might be especially well remunerated for delivering very high levels of growth, or rescuing a troubled company.
- Some companies benefit from an "implicit" government guarantee. It is difficult to quantify this benefit, as by definition it is vague and affects various sectors in different ways. With such a guarantee comes an enhanced ethical obligation to government.

- Investors achieve gains in a number of ways, including through capital gains.
- In countries with ostensibly similar risk profiles, the achievable return from similar asset classes can vary significantly.

Shareholders

Shareholders provide the equity (or risk capital) to start, run and grow a business. Equity capital must be present or committed in all normal situations before debt can be raised. Equity shareholders stand to gain most from a successful company, and lose most (their entire value) if it is unsuccessful. This position is unchanged between a private company (i.e. shares are not traded) and a publicly quoted company (shares are traded on an exchange) – the difference between a private company and a quoted company is the ability to easily buy or sell shares, which can be described as "liquidity."

In some companies, employees are remunerated in part with shares, aimed at aligning their interests with those of other shareholders. This is particularly relevant to senior employees, notably executive Board members.

The investment cycle and capital structure

Shareholder returns are normally seen in two ways: first, through the payment of dividends, and second through capital growth in the value of shares, referred to collectively as Total Shareholder Return (TSR). Which of these provides the returns is typically dependent on two factors: first, the capital requirements of the company, which relate to its level of growth and the sector in which it operates; and second, its capital structure – the balance of debt and equity in its financing.

Early stage or newly formed companies, typically going through relatively high levels of growth, would be expected to show returns through growth in share value, and not pay dividends. Conversely, companies which are in a mature stage of development and in relatively low-risk industries (such as utilities) would be expected to offer relatively high dividends and relatively low capital growth.

Companies will increase their intrinsic business risk by taking on debt, which is a form of liability. However, at the same time, given that debt will (in normal circumstances) benefit from a level of protection agreed by the company, it will be lower cost than funding with equity, and so overall can enhance returns to shareholders. As debt levels increase in a company (as a proportion of overall capitalisation), costs of debt will also increase.

Companies who finance and shareholders who finance businesses with unusual levels of debt are taking greater risks in order to augment their returns.

Assessing affordable dividends

Dividends can be assessed based on a "pay out ratio" or its inverse, "dividend cover." This is used to indicate the level of profit retained by a company for investment above its cost of depreciation. A lower dividend cover, or higher pay out ratio, will generally indicate that a company has less scope for reinvestment or organic growth from its existing business areas.

Consequently, a company not paying a dividend can be an indication of high growth, where the company will seek to reinvest its capital in its business, or alternatively (normally in a mature or low-growth sector) an indication that a company is troubled (e.g. is highly indebted, or has experienced a downturn in revenue).

Companies can also offer returns to shareholders in other ways, for example, by repurchasing and cancelling their own shares, which will be intended to augment the level of earnings (and therefore dividends) per share for remaining shareholders. This can also have the effect of holding up share prices, as there is a buyer of shares ready in the market (the company itself) in the event that share prices fall. Although the result of a share repurchase programme will be that total net income falls (due to the cost of financing the share repurchases), the net income calculated on a per share basis (normally referred to as Earnings Per Share or EPS) will increase. This type of financial engineering can have the effect of holding up company share prices, and therefore on a short term basis can be viewed favourably by companies and shareholders, although it may also have the effect of distorting equity related returns (and incentives for executives).

Dividend cover will vary in a range depending on the investment requirements and opportunities of a company. Typically, dividend covers of less than 1.5x net income will appear low, and risk a dividend cut at some stage. Equally, cover of above about 3x looks as though a company would have scope to increase dividends. It is difficult to make a clear explanation of the reasonable bands of dividend cover, as the range of related factors can be complex, relating to the requirements and opportunities facing an individual company.

There is an obvious iteration between dividends and reinvestment in a company. Companies require ongoing investment to maintain growth, and therefore value. Bonus pools in investment banks relate both to remuneration for the current year, and also investment in the business, as employees and their intellectual capital are in a real sense part of the capital of the business. The approach of banks which in years of poor financial performance sacrifice dividends in order to maintain (or lessen the reduction in) staff bonuses may be to a significant extent based on the need to preserve the value of the business. This will inevitably raise the question of whether the demands of high performing employees for high remuneration is reasonable. The risk of the loss of such staff, who are presumably motivated by financial rewards, can only be because they would leave for a "competitor" – this could be another bank, or it could be a private equity or *hedge fund*, or something similar. Leaving aside the question of the individual ethics, from a Board perspective (and Board members are typically not remunerated with bonuses), the question can be one not of "how do we justify this action" but "how do we present this." Management failures over time can contribute to this type of dilemma: a failure to invest in training of management and good management systems will exacerbate the risk of losing employees by poor and damaging succession planning. The feudal nature of management in many (most) investment banks contributes to this type of phenomenon. I observed a change, for example, in the type of individual appointed as head of research in investment banks, from senior research analysts who could mentor and train junior staff, to more charismatic individuals with a greater outward focus, which assisted in recruitment. One unintended consequence of such a change is the increased need to poach (politely termed a "lateral hire") employees from competitors, at higher salaries. This would be expected to tend to increase the salary level throughout a department, and if the pattern is repeated, throughout an organisation. A company has a duty to take into account the interests of its employees, and to support them appropriately. However, being an employee does not on its own result in sharing equity risk – either the downside or the upside.

The position of a company considering the trade-off between shareholder returns, notably in the form of dividends, and the state is inevitably more complex. First, because the company has a clear set of duties towards shareholders, whereas the nature of duties towards the state is more opaque – and can be difficult to identify due to differences in stated policy between ministers, and between governments of differing political complexions. In reality, company Boards need to a large extent to second guess what is in the interests of shareholders, and by the same token cannot clearly understand what is in a country's interests. Paying higher levels of remuneration will, in most cases, increase taxation. At the same time, it may contribute to criticism of a government, if not in actual civil unrest. Consequently, the nature of duties to government are of a different type than to shareholders: although a company's first duty is to its shareholders, a company must take note of its ethical duty to support its host government, and consider its actions regarding dividends and remuneration in the light of any concerns which might arise. This duty is more clearly one of avoiding harm, rather than positively contributing – it is not clear that a company should be actively seeking to enhance government policy, as this may at times be akin to taking political sides (although this may vary in some jurisdictions with high levels of continuity of government over long periods of time).

Based on a very long career in fund management, one long-standing and successful manager of charity and ethical funds, Bill Seddon of the Central Finance Board of the Methodist Church in the UK, believes that companies tend to hit major problems where they disproportionately favour one group above others, whether shareholders, employees or customers. This became the basis for a series of Affirmative funds: the Charity Commission wouldn't permit an ethically restrictive policy for a common investment fund open to all charities, so Seddon structured it positively on the basis of no one group of stakeholders gaining disproportionately over any other.

How should risk be shared and rewarded with employees and the state?

Shareholders can offer unusually high remuneration to executives in certain situations, notably very large companies, high growth and very troubled companies. This is because in each of these three situations, the option value of the equity is very high, and the decisions made by management and the actions they take can have a very significant influence on value. A company in a very low-risk environment, such as a utility, will typically expect to pay lower remuneration, as the executives have a less problematic task in managing a low-risk business.

In many cases where remuneration is unusually high, a high element of remuneration will consist of shares (or options to buy shares). Consequently, if the executive is successful and the share price increases, remuneration can be very high.

Where executives are remunerated in shares or share options, and high levels of remuneration result, it will normally be the case that a Board and shareholders have understood the prospect of employees achieving high rewards. This can, however, result in a situation where an executive or a group of executives can earn an unusual multiple of their normal remuneration. With equity-based remuneration, it is difficult to separate the performance of an executive from industry wide factors. For example, executives in the oil sector will benefit from the impact on their companies from a rise in oil prices, which will not purely relate to their own performance. Shareholders will also benefit from this, as will the state from increased taxation (if only on the increased remuneration). It will disbenefit consumers of oil, and if inequality of earnings and wealth is considered to be unethical, absent any redistributive taxation could be viewed as damaging for customers.

With tax breaks common for employees owning shares in the companies they work for, it would appear that from a public policy perspective, governments will often be aligned with shareholders in believing that it is beneficial for employees to be able to benefit from and be incentivised by owning shares in the companies for which they work.

The "implicit" government guarantee

Government will not, other than in exceptional cases, directly share business risks of private-sector companies. Government stands to increase taxes from growing companies. However, some factors can reduce tax payments from very successful companies. Notably, where a company is refinanced with debt, as interest payments on debt are treated for tax purposes as a cost, and therefore deducted from taxable profits, high levels of debt will reduce tax paid. Governments therefore incentivise companies to use debt. This releases equity to be redeployed by companies, or by their shareholders from the repayment of dividends. The limitation of this model comes from the internationalisation of investment, where shares (including controlling shareholdings) may be owned internationally, and consequently the dividends paid by a company may not result in taxation in the same country. There are countries – for example, India – where there are significant legal restrictions on how cross-border investment is regulated and structured. Attempts to limit cross-border ownership may be counterproductive in many circumstances hindering investment and growth.

Some companies and some industrial sectors may benefit from an "implicit" government guarantee. This was seen in many countries during the financial crisis within the banking sector. An *implicit government guarantee* has also been observed in many countries within automotive manufacturing, and would be expected across certain strategic industries, notably the utility sector. The existence of an implicit guarantee should provide a level of enhanced general ethical obligation to the government concerned, although it may not actually be clear that such a guarantee exists (it is only implicit), and whether the position of a company is different from many other companies. For example, whereas Citi Group benefited from US government support, Lehman did not. AIG was supported by the US government, but a significant UK insurance company, Equitable Life, did not benefit from government support when it became insolvent in 2000.

An implicit government guarantee is not firm in most situations, by definition. It raises the ethical obligation on a company in some way, which is difficult to measure. It is difficult to conclude that the possible existence of implicit expectation of government support should demand a change in company behaviour, if only because a company should in any case be acting to preserve and grow value for its shareholders, and to continue to serve its customers.

Leverage and shifting fiduciary duties

This will not, in almost all circumstances, conflict with its obligations to the state. The difference will exist when shareholders are seeking to increase returns by increasing leverage to imprudent levels. In this circumstance, shareholders may rebalance their risk by taking equity out of a business. The economic impact of this may be less in countries where bankruptcy protection is available, notably in the US, but greater where criminal penalties exist for "wrongful" trading or trading while insolvent, and therefore company directors are restricted from the ability to restructure financial liabilities. The copying of US-derived financial structures into markets without the same capability for *restructuring* as the US will lead to an increase in inherent risk. It is important therefore to realise that the ethical issues associated with increasing leverage are inevitably likely to vary depending on country, and will include a cognisance of the impact on the government of corporate failure. This can be a particular issue where a company issues "securitised" debt, which may be at a high ratio of loan amount to the company's value (known as a *LTV* ratio). As leverage increases, the amount of information required by lenders and contact with the company increases. There is an understanding in some jurisdictions, notably the US, that where a company enters the "zone of insolvency" its fiduciary duties shift from shareholders to all creditors.

Capital gains

Shareholder returns are made up of dividends – which are paid from the profits of a company, and gains on shares, ultimately by a sale of shares. Governments tend to favour share gains for most investors, by giving incentives for investors to achieve returns through appreciations in share prices. Taxation on capital gains is typically markedly different from taxation on income from dividends, (although this would not be the case in jurisdictions with a flat-tax regime). This is based on encouraging active use of capital to fund industrial growth, rather than any ethical view on the desirability of earning income from dividends rather than share sales.

What level of return is acceptable in the light of equity risk?

There is no single absolute level of risk premium which can be stated. The Equity risk premium is the return above the cost of low-risk government debt required to justify equity investment. The Equity Risk Premium will change over time, depending on the scale of available investment opportunities, and the alternative uses for capital. The cost of equity will also vary from country to country. In general, the equity return required in northern Europe has been significantly lower than in the US, for example, even where country credit ratings are very similar.

Risk has been mis-priced in many contexts, which typically has had significant public consequences. This was clearly the case with sub-prime mortgage lending, but equally was the case with the UK's early PFI (Private Finance Initiative) projects, where project returns were clearly very high compared with the risks associated with those projects. This resulted in a higher cost of essential public services than was necessary, imposing a burden on the taxpayer (although it is not possible to tell what the actual cost would have been under a different procurement programme, making the "burden" potentially only hypothetical).

A zero-sum game?

In a single year, a company has a finite amount of profits which can be used to remunerate employees, pay tax, and remunerate shareholders, both through paying dividends and reinvesting to grow the business.

Over time, a company's decisions as to how to treat employees, shareholders and the state will affect its profit growth. Decisions on how to treat different groups in an individual year must therefore be made based on an understanding of the overall implications of those decisions.

For example, when an investment bank suffers a poor year for overall profits, if it fails to remunerate individually successful traders, it may imperil its overall business model and long-term value – adversely affecting shareholders (who will see lower long term returns) and the state (who will see reduced taxation).

Conversely, if the investment bank consistently remunerates traders to an extent not justified by their performance, this will result in a long-term reduction in the value of the shareholders' interest in the company. This can happen in areas where it is difficult to assign an appropriate cost of capital to the use of the company's balance sheet, or where the risk associated with the activities is relatively high.

Judgements in this kind of area are rarely able to be made with precision at the time.

Sharing high risks, super-normal returns and pain

The position of equity shareholders is different from executives. Whereas executives have a contract giving them remuneration for services, equity shareholders own the capital required to enable a company to carry out its activities, and do not have contractual protection in the event of a downturn in performance.

Executives have an asymmetric risk profile – significantly higher upside than downside, especially if they are largely remunerated with equity. Nonetheless, salary packages provide protection against a significant level of risk.

Shareholders therefore typically stand to gain most in the event of high levels of success, and this includes employee shareholders – who tend to gain most when they own equity over sustained time periods, or during major transitions (*IPOs*, restructurings etc.).

In the event of the most serious kind of corporate problems, resulting in insolvency, typically the tax authorities and employees have a level of protection (although this varies between jurisdictions).

The type of financial gains arising from major transitions in a company's development can be very significant for investors, and for employee shareholders. This type of success can give rise to inequality among employees and among executives: an accountant in the finance department of a successfully IPO'd company may make a multiple of the income of a similarly qualified and diligent accountant in a different setting (such as a utility, or an equivalent company which does not go through an IPO). There may be an element of chance in an individual's economic success, regardless of their skill, application and ambition. Much ethical thinking, including Rawls' theory of justice suggests that provided this does not harm others, this is ethically permissible.

Equity shareholders take the greatest risk in their investment. Equity stands to be wiped out, whereas employees have a level of protection, creditors have first rights to a company's assets, and the state can receive taxes from "winners" from a bankruptcy (i.e. competitors).

Sectors

The starting point for many investors who focus on ethical issues is to review the actual activity of the company concerned, rather than its governance. The treatment of sector and activity specific issues has to be addressed to make an ethical policy effective and convincing (both to a Board and to its various stakeholders).

Ethical arguments for sector exclusions are advanced from both secular and religious based funds and organisations. There is a significant commonality between approaches to many high profile issues, especially to alcohol, tobacco and firearms, including across religious and secular ethical approaches. There are a number of specifically environmental funds (sometimes referred to as "sustainable" funds), which either screen out companies they consider irresponsible, or which invest only in technology aimed at abating climate change. As an example of a secular approach to ethical investment, one fund, the Quilter Cheviot Climate Asset Funds has three "macro drivers": climate change, resource scarcity and population growth.

There are some areas of activity where objections are only found from religious ethical concerns. Both Islamic and Jewish investment criteria will typically exclude investment in pork products, for example.

In reality, the ethical objections to some activities are heavily nuanced, especially with regard to alcohol and defence: for example, in many developing markets where clean water supplies are limited, the role of beer in society is different to that in areas with easily accessed supplies of clean water. A difference is sometimes drawn between "defensive" and "offensive" military equipment, and religious organisations do not simply exclude all firearms. Some Church-based investment organisations justify some level of involvement in defensive military equipment on the "Just War" theory, which is often identified with St Augustine of Hippo (354–430).

This does not mean that a company carrying out an intrinsically unethical activity – such as tobacco farming – cannot aim to do so with as much care regarding ethics as possible. Investors in these companies, who presumably do not share the ethical objections to the activities per se, perhaps by taking a (misplaced) ethical view very much focused on personal freedom of choice, should nonetheless continue to press for ethical behaviour in the way that activities are carried out.

The difficulty for investors including companies which invest in certain proscribed sectors isn't in the underlying rationale for doing so, although this is done with varying levels of sophistication. Instead it lies in applying judgement to what level of activity is acceptable: that is, when an investor avoids investment in companies selling tobacco, what level of tobacco sales would justify selling shares in a supermarket group? The thresholds for not investing in alcohol retailing vary between different funds. Exclusions can be based on any involvement, for example for offensive weapons, or on a wide range of thresholds for alcohol related activities (10 per cent to 25 per cent). As for judging levels of remuneration, ethical teaching is useful in understanding how to identify and view important questions, but judgement is required in assessing how to apply firm numbers in proposing answers.

It is difficult to see how any ethical framework adopted by the Board of a company could be worthwhile if it does not include as a major component a guide to deciding whether activities are ethical in themselves. This may perhaps be most relevant to new areas of investment, as in practice a company is unlikely to decide that existing core activities are simply unethical.

If, however, this were to happen, this would lead to an interesting question over how to manage the exit from an activity: can the activity ethically be sold, or must it be closed down with a potential loss of value to shareholders, and a resulting breach of fiduciary duties? During the apartheid government of South Africa in 1986, investors called on Barclays to exit their activities. This led to the sale (rather than closure) of Barclay's interest in its South African business. In other cases, such as Zimbabwe, there has been a mix of responses, with some ethical investors arguing against a withdrawal, due to concerns over the impact on employees locally.

To take the approach advocated in *De Oficiis* (Cicero), the honourable approach would be to close an unethical activity, and it can be argued that this is in line with duties to shareholders, as it protects shareholders against contingent risks associated with the sale of a business.

Trustees of purely secular funds – such as company pension funds – will typically ask about ethical issues in individual sectors – that is, taking as a starting point the same type of issues as those from specifically ethical backgrounds, albeit often with a less sophisticated philosophical underpinning. The level of basic investment training required to be appointed a trustee is surprisingly low (i.e. typically there is no specific education required, although many trustee bodies take advantage of training made available, typically by industry bodies or by investment managers).

Trustees of funds interested in ethics typically ask mainly about their sector exclusions. There is an increased focus on voting, which has grown substantially over the past five years or so. However, the level of thought going into this must be questioned: global investment portfolios will total investments in approx. 3,000 companies. Voting is delegated to specialist firms, who will ensure that shares are voted in line with established policies. This will have a base-level impact, but is short of the type of substantive engagement which is likely to change aberrant behaviour.

Conclusions

It is obvious that a company, in order to ensure its long-term success, should make appropriate decisions about how to deal with returns to shareholders, employees and the payment of taxes.

These decisions should be informed not just by financial considerations, but by clear ethical thinking, which in turn is necessary to ensure that mistakes are not made in the treatment of individual groups and the interplay between those groups.

It is apparent that companies and Boards of Directors often in practice use consequentialist reasoning to justify the ethics of their decisions and actions. However, without consideration of virtue and duty, ethical decisions are likely to be flawed.

It is difficult to ignore the ethical traditions valuing "freedom," from Augustine to Ayn Rand, whose theory of objectivism has set out *inter alia* to counter conventional objections to capitalism. However, the value of "freedom" is not unchallenged, and is at least implicitly questioned in more collectivist ethical frameworks.

Ethical thinking is essential in informing Board decisions on how profits are shared. No ethical framework in this context is uncontentious. What is most important is that a conscious effort should be made to think ethically, and the parameters used should be open.

Once a Board has understood and accepted the need for a clear ethical framework, the question which Boards should consider is this: should decisions be based on ethical principles clearly understood by investors, or by more populist ethical principles which would be publicly recognised as being ethical?

It is ethically tenable to set a framework based on Aristotelian and Kantian ethics – virtue and freedom. But, it would be risky. To take an approach which is focused overmuch on a company's duties to stakeholders other than its shareholders is also problematic: this risks violating concepts of personal freedom, and also conflates companies with the state – although the benefits of corporate activity benefit the state, the primary focus of a private company's activities will not be furthering the state. A company represents a set of specific interests of individuals, which choose to exercise these interests through the ownership of shares. The bifurcation of concern at *compensation* levels within publicly quoted companies, when compared with public fascination with entrepreneurial success shows the mercurial nature of popular – and therefore at least in part political – concern over remuneration.

Much political criticism of corporate behaviour – paying tax, remuneration – is questionable precisely because it is political. Comments about excess remuneration are made by politicians who earn considerable sums subsequent to their political careers. Criticism of hedge funds is made regardless of the facts, as it is politically expedient to do so. Tax is more vulnerable to populist political criticism than other areas, because it is the state's sole prerogative to levy and raise taxes.

10
Ethical Frameworks and Case Studies

He had bought a large map representing the sea,
Without the least vestige of land:
And the crew were much pleased when they found it to be
A map they could all understand

Lewis Carroll, The Hunting of the Snark

An understanding of ethics and using ethical principles is an important part of decision making, for an individual or for a company. There are different – sometimes conflicting – ethical principles, which can lead to varying decisions which are nonetheless ethical. It is important for a company to set out transparently how it identifies ethical problems and how it resolves them – including prioritising clear ethical rules. As will be seen from the case studies below, this may be more likely to change the way a decision is implemented than alter the decision itself.

Corporate codes of conduct and ethics tend to provide a general exhortation to be ethical or to avoid unethical behaviour, but can fall short of explaining how this should be approached in practice.

The attempt here is to provide a short set of ethical principles, based around a company's rights and duties, and to show how these could impact on decisions regarding how profits are shared between shareholder, state and employee.

Set out below are the ethical rights and duties, principles and suggested priorities for an ethical framework.

The framework takes clear ethical rights and duties into account, but then can be used to apply a different (or no) prioritisation. There is not necessarily a single correct framework which should be followed.

A series of hypothetical questions are answered using each of the frameworks, to show their similarities and differences in practice, relating to remuneration, tax and dividends.

By reviewing the ethical principles and priorities in the context of each case study, it is hoped that Boards can identify the different ethical approaches possible, and can test whether they are prepared to accept the implications of the ethical approach they would choose to follow. In addition, considering different rules or priorities will assist in understanding the basis for existing ethical considerations, and how these fit into ethics more broadly.

Ethical frameworks that are based solely or almost solely on one specific ethical tradition (notably either consequentialist or duty based) are likely to prove to be highly contentious – for example, a consequentialist approach is more likely to appear highly unethical from a political or popular perspective, whereas an entirely deontological approach is likely to undermine the requirements of equity investment by failing to recognise the uniquely risky position of shareholders. Any set of ethical rules/principles needs to be applicable to real world situations, but without resulting in the downward spiral of moral relativism.

These frameworks are consciously based on ethical thinking, and not legal or regulatory principles. There can be significant overlap in these areas, and it is acknowledged there are significant complexities of legislation between (and even within) countries. In practice, this book argues that there is an ethical duty tantamount to a *categorical imperative* to uphold the law of the country in which a company is operating, and this has the result that (i) where a legal requirement mandates a course of action outside the ethical framework, the law should be followed, but it should be acknowledged that it runs counter to the conclusion of ethical deliberations; alternatively (ii) if this accommodation is not acceptable, the company might in an extreme situation consider ceasing to operate in the country concerned. A distinction needs to be made between criminal and civil law; there may be also occasions where a breach of civil or criminal law is inevitable, and is not prevented by an ethical categorical imperative.

Such a breach would not undermine the government concerned. For example, where a company in the extractive industries acquires a mine or oilfield with a poor employment or safety track record, and changing its operations would take some time – such an acquisition could be ethically beneficial, but nonetheless would bring inevitable breaches of the law in some areas in the short term. As a result, a legal analysis of the implications of the investment might give a different answer from a purely ethical one.

Reconciling equality

There is a specific problem with equality of outcome (i.e. wealth inequality, income inequality) as opposed to equality of opportunity which should be compatible with management of a company. It is not feasible for a company to reconcile equality of outcome with the rights of shareholders and duties to other groups, including employees. The major ethical area of interest which can provide a specific problem in reconciling within a framework is equality: it has to either take precedence over the rights of shareholders to derive a return, or be subservient to it. If it is overridden by shareholder rights, then the need to have freedom to remunerate desired executives has to follow as ancillary to shareholder rights – but note, this has significant implications for what shareholder consent is required for executive remuneration. Consequently, equality becomes of a second order for the company. This does not mean that it is ignored, but it ends up placed within the area of government or wider societal concern. Mervyn King, former Governor of the Bank of England, writing in the *Telegraph* said: "Inequality does matter, and measures to reduce it have a proper place in economic policy. But by promoting efficiency and raising living standards, a market economy has proved its worth."[1]

Rights and duties

The different stakeholders in a company can be attributed specific rights:

1. Shareholders have the right to earn a return from investments.
2. The state has the right to levy taxes on profits earned by the company.

3. Employees have the right to be paid fairly, notably in line with their terms of employment.
4. Society more widely has the right to expect the company to behave responsibly.

These can also be expressed as duties:

1. The company has the duty to protect shareholders interests (which essentially means managing risk and return).
2. The company has a duty to support government in the countries in which it operates, including paying appropriate taxes.
3. The company has a duty to pay employees fairly.
4. The company has a broad duty as a corporate citizen.
5. The company has a duty to various counterparties, including customers, clients and suppliers.

Ethical principles

There are a series of thematic areas of ethics which will impact on identifying the rights and duties, and prioritising these, including:

Freedom: Although most obviously relating to the rights of shareholders to benefit from their investments, companies need to ensure that in exercising freedoms or rights of shareholders, they are not obstructing freedoms of other groups or duties to other groups.

Justice: Companies must take into account ideas of justice and fairness, in the light of the various rights and duties which affect them, including a clear duty to government – companies rely on stable government.

Equality: This is a difficult area to reach a clear conclusion which will be universally accepted. It is difficult for most companies to accept equality of wealth, income or outcome as a principle. Despite this, companies should be able to accept two concepts: first, the benefits of equality of opportunity; and second, the need to address widespread concerns regarding social and financial inequality, even if these concerns are not accepted per se.

Intention: The intent of a course of action being considered should be judged against its impact on the various identified rights and duties.

Consequences: The results of a decision need to be assessed in respect of any group which have rights, or to which the company owes duties, and can also be used to assess the "utility" of a course of action (the total benefit resulting from it).

Action: It is integral to the ethical value of an activity to understand what is being done, the intent and the consequences. This brings in Hindu and Buddhist ethical traditions very clearly, where it is the action itself which is most important to assess. For example, in a broader strategic sense this raises the question of what the company's funds are being invested to do.

Key questions

Within each of these ethical areas, there is a series of questions which can be asked:

- Who has rights to a share in profits?
- Who does the company have a duty to pay?
- Would any payments result in a reduction in the value of the company to its shareholders?
- Would any payment to shareholders unfairly disadvantage any other group to which the company has an ethical duty?

Overall, it is important to ask (i) what is the priority, and (ii) which of these rights or duties are categorical imperatives? That is to say, a rule might not be the first priority, but satisfying the rule might be an absolute or necessary condition for sharing profits.

Rules

Using the rights/duties, the rules and the questions outlined above, a series of ethical rules can be developed.

- *Shareholders*: Shareholders have a right to earn a return from their investments, including to reinvest in the business to create further value or to take out dividends, provided this does not conflict with the company's other ethical duties. In determining how to use profits, companies should not unfairly transfer wealth between groups.
- *Employees*: A company should deal fairly with all employees, including directors and executives. Executive remuneration should be fair, based on the required amounts for the job to be performed

well. Employees at all levels have a duty to respect the rights of shareholders, and not to abuse their positions. Remuneration which is not justified is an unethical transfer of value from shareholder to employee. Shareholder votes should not be a fait accompli. They should be meaningful, in the sense of allowing shareholders the ability to dissent with Board recommendations without resulting in the collapse of a Board (unless, of course, that is exactly what shareholders intend). This needs to take effect within the constraints of contract law – companies must be able to be trusted by those they do business with, which includes honouring contracts. In terms of remuneration, this means that companies should not seek a vote just on an entire remuneration report, but should put to a separate vote any unusual remuneration arrangements. Executives should be held to account where they fail to perform satisfactorily, and under such circumstances they should not profit from having failed to perform.

- *Government*: A company has a broad and clear ethical duty to support government. This includes paying appropriate taxes levied by governments. Companies should not be expected to second guess the spirit of legislation, but at the same time should not make use of obvious loopholes. This includes considering cases where changing global commerce has moved so fast as to outdate national and international legislative norms. Taxes due to the state should be paid, and tax structuring should:

  - Avoid obvious loopholes.
  - Avoid transfer pricing which misrepresents economic reality.
  - Avoid materially or systematically increasing business risk to an extent not explained to shareholders.
  - Avoid distorting reported profits, including to maximise remuneration.
  - Avoid breaking normally understood ethical rules – such as by lying.
  - Follow the letter of (and arguably the spirit of) the law.
  - Be transparent to the state (or states) concerned.

- *Other counterparties*: A company has a range of contractual obligations, such as to creditors and suppliers. Contracts are based on systematically describing a series of promises, which a company has an ethical obligation to honour, before shareholders can take *returns.* Companies should not make decisions on use of profits which would result in them breaching duties to these or other groups, including:

- *Suppliers*: A company's behaviour to its suppliers can be supportive of them, or can be abusive. Companies have an ethical duty to suppliers, and where the company has significant buying power, it should not use this power abusively.
- *Customers*: Although customers do not receive a share of profits, it must be accepted that a company has a duty of care to customers, and shareholders via the company should not seek to derive a profit through behaving unethically towards customers
- *Local communities*: The impact a company can have on a local community can be very beneficial, or it can destroy a community. Companies should respect the rights of local communities.
- *Contractors*: Companies will use specialist contractors to perform specialist functions, which will vary from the low-skilled, to the highly technical. Companies have a duty of care to contractors as well as to employees.

Implementing these rules requires identification of which rules will take priority, and which are inviolable. The two things are different: an inviolable rule can result in courses of action being blocked, even if it is not a priority.

In most cases, in apportioning profits it is probable that the rights of shareholders will be prioritised, followed by an inviolable rule of duty to employees and government.

Alternative ethical frameworks

The different priorities given can be varied based on considerations of a relatively small number of key ethical factors:

- *Shareholder rights and freedom*: Are shareholder rights to make a return superior to all other rights and duties relating to the company? In which case, the only practical constraints are those of a *utilitarian* nature.
- *Ethical duties*: Does the company understand and accept a range of ethical duties to groups other than shareholders?

- *Specific duty to government and the state*: Does the company accept there is a specific duty to the state, including to pay appropriate taxes?
- *Employees*: Are proposals for employee remuneration fair, and do they avoid unjustified transfer of value from shareholders to employees?
- *Justice and equality*: Is inequality accepted as a specific ethical concern? In which case, there are significant constraints around remuneration and tax.
- *Virtue*: Are there actions which the company believes are positive, which should be required of executives and employees and can be furthered through the *distribution* of profits? These could include, for example, wage restraint, or socially responsible activities such as supporting schools in deprived areas local to where the company operates.
- *Utilitarian/consequentialist*: What are the direct and indirect consequences of the decision, and are the indirect consequences something which should be taken into account? The purely utilitarian framework would have some elements in common with each of the others: along with justice, it will take into account indirect effects; along with freedom, it will not look at issues which are clearly outside the company's control.
- *Action*: Is the activity being contemplated – notably in this context from reinvestment in a company – in an area which in itself raises ethical concerns?

Prioritising

Depending on which of these elements are accepted by the company, ethical rules can be prioritised differently.

This can have different results, at least in theory:

- An ethical framework based on *equality* has a high risk of incompatibility with either the concept of shareholder rights or of the concept of capital carrying a cost or of being rationed. Attempts to specifically equate executive remuneration to causes of chronic inequality are not sufficiently convincing to justify Boards of companies altering their behaviour to treat relative inequality as a priority.

- Alternatively, a company with an ethical framework based solely on *freedom* will risk failing to take into account key issues surrounding the rights of non-shareholder groups nonetheless directly affected by its actions, and therefore risk incurring popular and political opposition to its actions.

The priority accorded to government

A company having regard to the position of the state, via taxation, should not view this in the same light as its relation to shareholders. A government's rights can be seen as stemming from the rights given to it by its citizens, which constitute its duties. This does not parallel the situation with the rights of an individual. A company is in the main acting on behalf of shareholders, which are ultimately an aggregation of the specific interests of individuals. Just as it is reasonable for a government to have regard to the wellbeing of its own citizens as a greater priority than the citizens of other countries, so a company can reasonably have regard to the interests of its own shareholders.

The company's attitude to taxation should take into account appropriate concern for the state, but it remains difficult for the company to second guess legislation, given that in so many arenas legislation is extremely technical (notably with regard to tax), and that in many contexts corporate taxation is used as a source of comparative advantage between governments.

The priority accorded to employees

The position of shareholders versus employees is complex, as employees have the right to be paid for their work, which may be protected from shareholders, depending on the jurisdiction. The treatment of shareholders versus employees should take into account an understanding of fairness, as well as an understanding of the rights of shareholders. This should include the position of executives, who in most cases are the custodians of the interests of shareholders, but cannot be so where their own remuneration is concerned due to the inherent *conflict of interest*.

Consequently, there are two separate issues: first, protecting shareholders from excessive remuneration of executives, and second, protecting other employees from unfair employment practices by the company as represented by its executives. The first of these is managed through the medium of Boards, and specifically of remuneration committees, and also in many cases by shareholder voting.

Shareholders and fund managers

Moves to strengthen the power of shareholders are of great importance. However, it is the position of fund managers which therefore requires scrutiny, given that they tend to be the representatives of large shareholders. Where the exercise of discretion by the shareholder is lacking, there is a significantly heightened risk of abuse. In turn, where a business is very large and complex, it may be simply impossible for Boards to fully assess the performance of individual executives.

Ratios

This can, as some suggest, be dealt with through applying ratios to executive pay. Such an approach will always be imperfect and give rise to (often unpleasant) perverse incentives.

An additional or alternative solution is to view remuneration as an ethical issue, subject to screening under an ethical framework with greater sophistication than saying that, for example, the remuneration of the CEO should be no more than 40x average pay.

The way ethical questions are handled is the key

Ethical consideration must take into account the real business issues in order to come to a justified conclusion – commercial issues are an intrinsic part of the ethical considerations.

In many cases, as will be seen in the case studies, the outcome of ethical deliberation will not directionally change the pragmatic outcome. However, asking the ethical questions appears likely to prompt changes in the way a resolution is implemented.

Worked examples/case studies

Set out below are a series of situations, where the possible outcome is assessed using each of the ethics frameworks above.

These situations are closely based on actual areas of concern, to investigate whether applying different ethical frameworks can give different outcomes to complex issues.

For these purposes, the ethics framework is assumed to be applicable for a Board and its committees, although it is possible that, for example, a Remuneration Committee could adopt a more detailed set of ethical principles to apply in specific circumstances (which would then cause a complication if it were not in accord with that of the Board).

As set out at the start of this book, the use of ethics can be helpful in prioritising rights and duties, but it is not easily adapted to consider specific numbers or formulae. Instead, it can provide a framework for decisions, and highlight areas of complexity and risk. The frameworks work on the basis of prioritisation of identified areas, in line with the thinking of philosophers as distinct as Rawls and Cicero.

Cast study 1: remuneration

Situation

A bank is faced with a choice regarding remuneration for employees in its *investment banking* division.

The bank is subject to close shareholder and public scrutiny. Performance has been relatively poor, but is on an improving trend.

A number of highly successful bankers are clearly prepared to leave their employment if they are, as they see it, "paid below market," and treated outside the at least implied norms as to how they would expect this employer to treat them.

However, the overall performance of the bank does not obviously justify an increase in remuneration. In theory at least the increase in bonus pool could be alternatively applied to increasing dividends. It should be noted that such an increase in dividends might be a one-off event, as without retaining the employees concerned underlying business performance would be unlikely to justify ongoing higher dividends.

The Board is faced with a choice: increase remuneration, which will be divisive with shareholders and attract negative media comment, potentially damaging the bank's reputation. Alternatively, the bank can reduce or maintain remuneration, which will result in a loss of key staff, and the probable loss of both profitable business and shareholder value.

Ethical considerations

Duties: The banks' primary duty is to shareholders – the interest of shareholders will be damaged if highly successful bankers are not retained. The bank will also have duties to other groups, notably employees, customers and the state. Part of these duties will be to ensure that remuneration is fair to all employees – this does not equate to needing to treat all employees equally.

Shareholder rights: Under the scenario where shareholder rights take clear precedence, there is nothing in the Board's duties which undermines an increase in remuneration, if this is supported by shareholders. As the payment is unusual – reflecting an increase in the normal pay out ratio – it may be reasonable for this to be proposed to shareholders provided that it is to be voted on as a separate resolution, rather than as part of a remuneration report. This raises the question of what would be the result if it were rejected.

Duty to government: This is particularly relevant in the case of remuneration in jurisdictions where the level of tax on remuneration exceeds corporation tax, and therefore the state is an actual beneficiary of increased remuneration. However, this raises the question of the conflicting interests of the state: over some timescales, social cohesion may be considered to be more important than maximising tax receipts. It is not possible – or appropriate – for companies to second guess the optimal solution for the state. Comparisons with tax on dividends also become probably too complex to assess, given the varying tax status of different investors (on-shore vs off-shore, pension funds which typically are tax-exempt etc.).

Duty to employees: The bank's duty to employees needs also be considered in this context: if the bank has made clear that bonuses will be calculated (as is the norm) on a simple pay out ratio basis, then it may be ethically obligated to make the payments. However, if the bank has been clear that payment depends on firm profitability (which is also common), then increased payments may not be ethically required. A variation comes in between remuneration paid by a profitable bank (i.e. sharing profits), compared with a loss-making bank. In this situation, rather than sharing profits, shareholders are being asked to invest. Consideration of ethical issues on a duty-based and virtue-based approach does not assist in assessing how much is enough or how much is too much in remuneration, where other employee groups are not disadvantaged by a decision.

Other duties: The question is what amount of care is taken to manage other interest groups, so as to avoid damaging the bank's reputation and therefore its value. If this cannot be managed, then an increase in remuneration may prove actually counterproductive, resulting in a reduction in value, and therefore in order to preserve shareholders' interests remuneration should not be increased. A duty-based approach which does not take into account commercial considerations must be flawed.

Justice and equality: The bank is proposing to increase investment in the business (as a proportion of profits), which will accrue to the benefit of the shareholders generally, but disproportionately to a specific group of employees. The group of employees have merited the proposed payment based on their business performance, and the proposed remuneration is on average at the low end of the normally accepted range for such performance.

Consequences: Countering this is the risk of adverse impacts on the bank, from (i) political interference, and (ii) loss of customers. If there is no real evidence that customers leave a bank because of remuneration issues, or that there is any punitive government action against the bank, then it is not possible to conclude that the high remuneration should be withheld. However, if the realistic consequence is that shareholder dissatisfaction will result in damage to the bank's overall reputation, and the loss of employees despite the increased incentive payments, then the result will look unethical from a consequentialist perspective.

Prioritisation

In this situation, the position of shareholders and the duty to employees do not necessarily conflict.

This is largely a business, and not an ethical decision, for the bank relying on a judgement on (i) the likelihood of employees departing, and (ii) the risk of a shareholder "revolt" (i.e. a significant proportion of shareholder voting against the proposal).

The ethical situation vis-à-vis the employees is also interesting: while employees may consider they have an implicit agreement with their employer, and so are entitled to leave their employer if not paid at full market rates, at the same time this view is a narrow one, and does not take into account the broad duty an employee has to an employer and its shareholders.

It is difficult to see circumstances where duties to other stake-holders can outweigh the duty to shareholders where no direct harm is caused to other groups of stakeholders.

There is no adverse direct impact on government from either decision, (although tax receipts will vary depending on how the company deals with a range of subsequent issues).

Circumstances where a change in prioritisation would change the outcome

The rights of shareholders appear to be best protected by increasing the incentivisation pool, but at the same time the reaction of a substantial number of shareholders risks rendering this strategy counterproductive. As is classically the problem with Utilitarianism, it is very difficult to prescribe what will make people happy.

Case study 2: CEO pay

Situation

A media company is negotiating a remuneration package for an internal candidate to promote to become CEO.

The previous CEO received a remuneration package of approximately 100 per cent more than the candidate's current package.

Executive pay and wealth inequality are major issues, and the company has been warned by its media advisors that a proposal to increase the candidate's pay will be made a leading news story, and bring significant political criticism and comment.

If the pay package is demonstrably below market levels, this poses two risks: first, the ethical risk of being unfair to the executive; and second, the risk of highlighting the capability of the executive, and a reason for other companies to believe they may be able to recruit him, thereby creating a potentially unstable environment.

When might this be appropriate: at a time when an executive is untried, with an acceptance that remuneration could be reviewed subsequently. The structure of incentivisation becomes crucial in this kind of situation. The limitation of equity based pay is that it can be uncapped, potentially exacerbating rather than reducing popular concern about remuneration. Many executives actively seek opportunities which are largely equity based, as these can be the best structure to earn high amounts over a period of time.

Ethical considerations

Shareholder rights: Shareholders' primary interest is that the company should be well run – which means it should show an increase in value over time, and that returns should be at or above industry norms without taking unusual risks. Increasing remuneration for the CEO, notably subject to appropriate safeguards (i.e. payments strictly limited if the CEO's contract is terminated) should not be ethically contentious. A Board's duty to shareholders requires appointing a capable CEO. This may mean recruiting an executive with an established track record and therefore paying a considerable premium.

Duty to employees: A company has a duty to pay an employee fairly (and takes a risk if it does not – that the employee leaves). If a CEO, once they have been in post for a relatively short period, is remunerated substantially below market levels, they become potentially under-remunerated, and unfairly remunerated.

Duty to government: There should be no especial political concerns, unless the remuneration of the outgoing CEO was an especially sensitive subject from a political perspective. The duty to political and popular opinion is harder to define than the duty to shareholders: the practice of politicians is not necessarily to maintain consistency in approach, and to reserve the right to change opinion. It is certainly not clear that political opposition to high remuneration for successful CEOs results in costly political entanglements, lost opportunities or other government-inspired actions against a company.

Other Duties: Other groups are unlikely to be adversely affected by this issue, unless the CEO's appointment is at an excessive cost, or the appointment turns out to be poor (and thereby damages the business, affecting suppliers, broader numbers of employees etc.). In this case, such duties are aligned with those to shareholders.

Justice and equality: If the candidate was selected through a fair process, reviewing internal and external potential CEOs, then this will satisfy the ethical need for the company to consider equality of opportunity, although there is an implication that recruitment at more junior levels should also be fair for this conclusion to be valid.

Consequences: The company needs to have a capable CEO in place. Provided a remuneration package does not (i) create reputational damage, or (ii) transfer unwarranted value from shareholders to the employee, there is no adverse consequence from most ethical perspectives. Based on utilitarian principles alone, remuneration could be agreed to in order to ensure continuity, or could be reduced, to avoid reputational damage and avoid higher pay outs thereby preserving more value for shareholders.

Prioritisation

Recruitment is not a precise exercise. An overpaid unsuccessful CEO is a double hit on shareholders, both costing money and (much more costly) losing value from poor judgement and/or execution. The level of remuneration is likely to have a minor impact compared with poor performance (or an adverse business environment). Separating out the impact of a change in business environment from the influence of an executive is frequently problematic in other than extreme circumstances. It is, for example, clearly easier to successfully grow the income of an oil company during a period of rising oil prices than one of falling prices. Napoleon's famous preference for lucky generals is also appropriate to corporate CEOs.

Duty-based and rights-based frameworks tend to give the same answers on this issue as utilitarian. It is when looking specifically from an equality perspective that problems emerge. These are ethical issues which cannot be resolved by rigorously looking at duties and rights. Many moral philosophers see equality of opportunity as being a desirable goal, rather than equality of resources. However, as set out above there is a view that equality of opportunity is lost from extremes of inequality in resources, even where opportunity is supposedly available equally.

The implication of this is that either (i) the identification of duties and rights is lacking a crucial element, or (ii) the argument from equality is in large part misplaced. It is difficult to see that this dilemma is capable of simple resolution, as the available solutions to the dilemma are incompatible with each other. These solutions are: analysis of ethical duties and rights relating to a company typically understates the importance of the state and groups such as employees; alternatively, that the argument from equality really relates to a type of attempted grab for someone else's property.

In a statist country, such as France, the former of these arguments may be seen as having credence. However, this implies that personal property has significant restrictions (i.e. it is only personal property to the extent allowed by the state), or that the state and society are undermined by high levels of inequality of resources.

If this latter is accepted, there is a further significant difficulty in deciding what level of differentiation in resource gives rise to an unethical outcome, and in deciding who can legitimately provide this assessment.

Given that there is no simple resolution to the dilemma between equality and freedom, for practical purposes it appears that a company considering ethical issues relating to executive remuneration should take into account the question of whether a remuneration package could undermine societal cohesion and government. Absent a specific and unusual reason for doing so, trying to identify any specific quantification of this appears to be at best totemic, if not creating perverse incentives and therefore risking causing harm.

Circumstances where a change in prioritisation would change the outcome

Having regard to the concerns of government, and concerns of shareholders of the risk of possible over-remuneration, would suggest it would be appropriate to structure the remuneration for the CEO candidate significantly towards performance, by using equity as a major part of the remuneration package, which would vest over time. This has the advantage that, as the CEO's reputation increases, it becomes more expensive for a competitor to try to recruit the CEO, due to the need to buyout higher amounts of equity.

Cast study 3: structured tax

Situation

A company's tax advisors come to them with a proposal to take advantage of existing legislation to reduce their tax bill when financing a major acquisition. This is brought to the Board by the Finance Director (or CFO) for consideration, and includes two alternatives:

The effect of the first structure would be to reduce the effective tax rate (ETR) by one per cent, from 26 per cent to 25 per cent. With a £400 million tax bill, this would reduce taxation by £4 million for an estimated five year period. The fees for setting up and maintaining the structure would be £250,000. The impact of this structure will be to increase earnings by £4 million or 0.26 per cent. This will not be sufficient to materially alter the market valuation of the company and therefore effect executive remuneration, or alter reported earnings sufficiently to affect executive remuneration.

The effect of the second structure would be to take the full benefit of the structure over a single year – that is, £20 million, after which the company's tax (and earnings) would revert to the normal structure. This would increase earnings by 1.25 per cent for one year.

As part of established procedures, all such structures must be disclosed to the tax authorities. This would be carried out in this case.

This structure would also move a proportion of the tax paid from the head office to the lower tax environment where the acquisition target is based.

Ethical considerations

Shareholders rights: The company has a duty to shareholders, which would suggest that where costs can be reduced it is beneficial to the interest of shareholders. The company should ensure that such a transaction does not in itself, or in combination with other measures, result in an unjustified payment to the executives of the company.

Duty to employees: It is difficult to see that the interest of employees could be harmed by reducing the effective tax rate, as this would give funds which could be allocated in part to reinvestment in the business.

Duty to government: It is important to avoid too broad or too pedantic an approach, given the sophistication of tax rules, compared with the broad nature of duties to government. If this is a well-understood structure, disclosed to the tax authorities, then if appropriate the government would be able to act to close the loophole (if that is what is the basis for the approach). If, on the other hand, this relates to an incentive for R&D activity designed to encourage investment, then the structuring would be warranted: there can be good and bad tax structuring from an ethical as well as an accounting perspective.

Duty based: The duty to shareholders can be in conflict with the duty to support the state. There is also a conflict between interests owed to different states. A multinational company may have a head office in one country – such as the US – but have operations in different countries. There may be scope to make decisions about how much of the finished product is manufactured in different jurisdictions, as well as some uncertainty or flexibility within the realm of transfer pricing.

Justice and equality: Fundamentally, ethical demands of justice and equality require a company to pay taxes, to contribute to the provision of the services which provide the environment in which the company can operate. It is difficult to state ethically what a tax rate should be, and how the company's *ETR* should correspond with headline levels of corporate tax, which will in many cases be affected by tax incentives, for example relating to research or new investment in fixed assets. While a company can seek to promote general social goods, it is not in the position of a charity or government. In theory, a company could dedicate all its resources to supporting a state, but this would undermine its ability to secure capital to operate and grow its activities.

How far could a company reduce its ETR without risking unethical behaviour? Is it up to the company to decide this, or is this the role of the tax authorities? In other words, the company should seek to manage its tax rate transparently taking advantage of tax legislation, and the tax authorities can change rules and legislation if required.

This, however, leaves scope for abuse. In reality, tax advisors would be more likely to present a range of options to the tax department of a large company, which would vary in how "aggressive" they are. At that stage, the tax advisors may be abnegating responsibility for the ethics of a decision, although clearly they would be ethically (and potentially legally) culpable if any structure was not legitimate.

The position of tax authorities is also complex: taxation is demonstrably used as a source of attracting investment, as well as to raise money to operate government departments and provide services.

Prioritisation

Consideration of the proposal needs to take account of the net impact on shareholders, rather than on earnings. Any increased pay out to executives will need to be included as part of this consideration. However, in such a large company, there are sufficient moving parts that pining down financial results to a single tax structuring will be problematic.

Circumstances where a change in prioritisation would change the outcome

A change in decision could be made depending on the threshold of confidence in the appropriateness of the tax structuring: if satisfying the duty to government were an inviolable rule, or being confident that the tax structure were within the spirit of the tax legislation.

It is not the ethical duties that are difficult to identify here, but the tests and levels within the understanding of tax treatment, as well as safeguards against profits being moved between years purely to hit targets for executive remuneration. The reduction in corporate tax rates makes this less likely: given a company with a 20 per cent effective tax rate, a 4 per cent change in ETR would be required to move earnings by 1 per cent.

A company cognisant of its ethical duties to shareholders and to government would wish to ensure that (i) the tax treatment did not act so as to trigger very high rewards for executives which would not otherwise be paid, resulting in a biased approach to considering the proposal; and (ii) that the tax treatment was not simply technically legitimate, and was not the result of an accidental glitch in a complex piece of legislation.

Postscript

*If I can't make it through one door, I'll go through another door—
or I'll make a door. Something terrific will come no matter how
dark the present.*

Rabindranath Tagore (1861–1941)

Business can play a major role in establishing strong ethical principles,
but cannot do so in isolation from the rest of society. This extends
to the impact of business being able to assist in reducing poverty
and promoting equality of opportunity. There are well recorded
instances of poor decision making, plainly unethical actions, and
abuse of communities by businesses.There are two issues which are
poorly understood but vitally important in the ethical position of
business: the methodology of investment decisions, and the extent
of the reliance of business on the rule of law. The well established
and almost globally used financial principles relating to investment
decisions – by institutional investors and by companies – are in
themselves consistent with the ethical duties on companies, and in
fact provide a foundation for business to be a proponent of strong
ethical values, especially equality and justice.The ethical duties of a
company and its shareholders to governments are profound. A large
company cannot operate and grow without the benefit of stability,
a range of social goods – for example education – and the preservation of contract law and limited liability. This has profound consequences from both a utilitarian and deontological perspective.This
book has argued that globalisation and the internet have not just

fundamentally changed government, but have fundamentally changed relations between the multinational company and governments, individually and internationally. This process has not reached a position where it is stable. It will change further. It is of course difficult to say how, but it is possible to see different responses: governments which clamp down on corporate behaviour; and governments which liberalise tax further and use it as a tool for gaining comparative advantage.When companies can site customer-facing activities, research and manufacturing in different locations, investment decisions become very competitive. Companies require access to highly educated and trained employees, R&D capability, very reliable infrastructure and communications, multi-lingual people. Education, training and infrastructure require expenditure and stability. This will set a minimum level of requisite taxation to support activities, but may not continue to support high spending programmes. This may not sit well with many high welfare spending governments. It is unfortunately difficult to see how the eradication of inequality sits easily with this view, as an aim or as a result.

Glossary

2 + 20: fee structure typically used by hedge funds whereby a 2 per cent base fee is levied on funds under management and 20 per cent of the upside or profit is paid

The 99%: reference to a slogan of the Occupy Movement, differentiating themselves from the 1 per cent who they claim have benefited from government largesse

Abrahamic faiths: collective term for Judaism, Christianity and Islam, relating to their historic and theological origins

Adviser: an Investment Banking or Financial Adviser giving advice primarily related to valuation, assisting with negotiation, co-ordinating due diligence and project management

Agent: an investment bank trading in the market on behalf of a client and typically receiving a commission

AGM: the annual general meeting of a company

Arranger: individual or group, usually an investment bank, charged with arranging finance for a transaction. Arranging finance would consist of preparing presentations to potential funders and securing financing (normally debt, but this can also include additional sources of equity finance)

Business ethics: an ethical understanding of business, applying moral philosophical principles to commerce

Capital markets: collective term for debt and equity markets; reference to the businesses within an investment bank which manage activity in the capital markets

Casino capitalism: term used to describe high risk investment banking activities with an asymmetric risk profile

Categorical imperative: the concept, developed by Immanuel Kant, of absolute moral rules

CDS (credit default swap): a form of financial insurance against the risk of default of a named corporation

CEO (chief executive officer): the most senior executive officer in a corporation

Church Investors' Group (or CIG): a group of the investment arms of a number of church denominations mainly from the UK and Ireland

Code of ethics: an investment bank's statement of its requirements for ethical behaviour on the part of its employees

Compensation: investment banker's remuneration or pay

Compliance: structures within an investment bank to ensure adherence to applicable regulation and legislation

Conflict of interest: situation where an investment bank has conflicting duties or incentives

Credit rating: an assessment of the creditworthiness of a corporation or legal entity given by a credit rating agency

CSR: corporate social responsibility

Derivative: a security created out of an underlying security (such as an equity or a bond), which can then be traded separately

Dharma: personal religious duty, in Hinduism and Buddhism

Discounted Cash Flow Valuation (DCF): the sum of

- the Net Present Value (NPV) of the cash flows of a company over a defined timescale (normally ten years);
- the NPV of the Terminal Value of the company (which may be the price at which it could be sold after ten years); and
- the existing net debt of the company.

Distribution: the marketing of securities

Dodd-Frank Act: the Dodd-Frank Wall Street Reform and Consumer Protection Act

Downgrade: a reduction in the recommended action to take with regard to an equity; or a reduction in the credit rating of a corporation

Duty-based ethics: ethical values based on deontological concepts

EBITDA: Earnings before Interest Tax Depreciation and Amortisation

EIAG: the Ethical Investment Advisory Group, of the Church of England

Encyclical: official letter from the Pope, to bishops, priests, lay people and people of goodwill

Enterprise Value (EV): value of an enterprise derived from the sum of its financing, including equity, debt and any other invested capital, which should equate to its DCF value

ETR: effective tax rate

EV:EBITDA: ratio used to value a company

Exit: sale of an investment

Financial adviser: see *Adviser*

Free-ride: economic term for gaining a benefit from another's actions

Glass-Steagall: the 1933 Act which required a separation of investment and retail banking in the US

Golden rule: do to others as you would have them do to you

Hedge fund: an investment fund with a specific investment mandate and an incentivised fee structure (see *2 and 20*)

High Yield Bond: debt sold to institutional investors which is not secured (on the company's assets or cash flows)

HMRC: Her Majesty's Revenue and Customs, the UK's authority for collecting taxes

Implicit government guarantee: belief that a company or sector benefits from the likelihood or Government intervention in the event of crisis, even though there are not formal arrangements for this to be the case

Insider dealing: trading in shares in order to profit from possessing confidential information

Insider trading: see *insider dealing*

Integrated bank: a bank offering both commercial and investment banking services

Integrated investment bank: an investment bank both active in capital markets and providing advisory services

Internal Rate of Return (IRR): the annualised return on equity invested. Calculated as the discount rate that makes the Net Present Value of all future cash flows zero

Investment banking: providing specialist investment banking services to large clients (corporations and institutional investors), including capital markets activities and M&A advice

Investment banking adviser: see *Adviser*

IPO: initial public offering

Islamic banking: banking structured to comply with Shariah (Islamic) law

Junior Debt: debt that is subordinated or has a lower priority than other debt

Junk bond: see *High Yield Bond*

Lenders: providers of debt finance

Leverage: debt

Leveraged acquisition: an acquisition of a company using high levels of debt to finance the acquisition

LIBOR: London Inter-Bank Offered Rate, the rate at which banks borrow from other banks

Liquidity: capital required to enable trading in capital markets

LTV: the Loan to Value ratio, a ratio used in analysing loans

M&A: mergers and acquisitions; typically the major advisory department in an investment bank

Market abuse: activities which undermine efficient markets proscribed under legislation

Market capitalism: a system of free-trade in which prices are set by supply and demand (and not by government)

Market maker: a market participant who offers prices at which it will buy and sell securities

Mis-selling: describing inaccurately securities (or other products) which are being sold

Moral hazard: the risk that an action will result in another party behaving recklessly

Moral relativism: the concept that morals and ethics are not absolute, and can vary between individuals

Natural Law: the belief that there is a universal moral code

Net assets: calculated as total assets minus total liabilities

Net Present Value (or NPV): sum of a series of cash inflows and outflows discounted by the return that could have been earned on them had they been invested today

NYSE: New York Stock Exchange

Operating profit: calculated as revenue from operations minus costs from operations

P:E: ratio used to value a company where P (Price) is share price and E (Earnings) is earnings per share

Price tension: an increase in sales price of an asset, securities or a business resulting from a competitive situation in an auction

Principal: equity investor in a transaction

Principal investment: proprietary investment

Private fquity: equity investment in a private company

Private equity fund: investment funds which invest in private companies

Proprietary investment: an investment bank's investment of its own capital in a transaction or in securities

Quantitative easing: government putting money into the banking system to increase reserves

Regulation: legal governance framework imposed by legislation

Restructuring: investment banking advice on financial restructuring of a company unable to meet its (financial) liabilities

Returns: profits

Rights-based ethics: ethical values based on the rights of an individual, or an organisation

Sarbanes Oxley: the US "Company Accounting Reform and Investor Protection Act"

SEC: the Securities and Exchange Commission, a US regulatory authority

Senior debt: debt that takes priority over all other debt and which must be paid back first in the event of a bankruptcy

Shariah finance: financing structured in accordance with Shariah or Islamic law

Socially Responsible Investing (SRI): an approach to investment which aims to reflect and/or promote ethical principles

Sovereign debt: debt issued by a Government

Speculation: investment which resembles gambling; alternatively, very short-term investment without seeking to gain management control

Spread: the difference between the purchase (bid) and selling (offer) price of a security

Subordinated debt: see *Junior debt*

Syndicate: group of banks or investment banks participating in a securities issue

Syndication: the process of a group of banks or investment banks selling a security issue

Utilitarian: ethical values based on the end result of actions, also referred to as consequentialist

Volcker Rule: part of the Dodd-Frank Act, restricting the proprietary investment activities of deposit taking institutions

Write-off: reduction in the value of an investment or loan

Zakat: charitable giving, one of the five pillars of Islam

Notes

1 Introduction and Summary

1. http://www.justice.gov/iso/opa/ag/speeches/2014/ag-speech-1405192. html (accessed 21 May 2014).
2. Mark 12:17
3. S. Green (2009) *Good Value: Reflections on Money, Morality and an Uncertain World* (London: Allen Lane).
4. J. Reynolds and E. Newell (2012) *Ethics in Investment Banking* (London: Palgrave Macmillan).
5. W. Temple (1984) *Christianity and Social Order* (London: Shepheard-Walwyn, New Edition 1984).

2 Greed and Self-Interest? Criticism of Corporate Decisions on Sharing Profits

1. Andrew Ross Sorkin, "What Timothy Geithner Really Thinks" *New York Times*, 8 May 2014.
2. T. Geithner (2014) *Stress Test: Reflections on Financial Crises* (New York: Crown Publishing Group).
3. http://www.washingtontimes.com/news/2014/may/9/bill-clinton-shocks-quip-goldman-sachs-ceo-slit-hi/#ixzz31i6cLx5s (accessed 14 May 2014).

3 Examining the Issues

1. http://www.standardlifeinvestments.com/exported/pdf/CG_Barclays_AGM_Statement/CG_Barclays_AGM_Statement_14.pdf (accessed 4 September 2014).
2. http://www.independent.co.uk/news/business/barclays-wins-shareholder-vote-over-pay-9281486.html (accessed 4 September 2014).
3. http://www.publications.parliament.uk/pa/cm201314/cmselect/cmpubacc/uc112-i/uc11201.htm, (16 May 2013, Q218 (accessed 4 May 2014).
4. http://www.oecd.org/tax/beps-about.htm (accessed 18 April 2014).
5. http://www.oecd.org/tax/C-MIN(2013)22-FINAL-ENG.pdf (accessed 17 April 2014).

4 Putting Business Ethics into Context

1. http://www.tescoplc.com/files/pdf/reports/tesco_and_society_2013_ipad. pdf (accessed 5 May 2014).
2. http://www.corporatereport.com/walmart/2014/grr/index.html (accessed 5 May 2014).

5 Applying Business Ethics

1. G. Cohen (2008) *Rescuing Justice and Equality* (Harvard: Harvard University Press).
2. I. Kant (1893) *Metaphysik der Sitten* 6: 325–28 (Berlin: Heimann).
3. For a more detailed summary of each of the ethical traditions, see Reynolds and Newell, *Ethics in Investment Banking*, chapter 3.
4. Kant (1970) *Kant's Political Writings*, ed. H. S. Reiss (Cambridge: Cambridge University Press).

6 Shareholders and Returns

1. http://www.laphamsquarterly.org/roundtable/roundtable/greatest-of-all-time.php (accessed 13 May 2014).

7 Employees and Remuneration

1. D. Kahneman (2011) *Thinking Fast and Slow* (London and New York: Allen Lane).
2. Quoted in *The Telegraph*, 4 March 2014.
3. "The Kay Review of UK Equity Markets and Long-Term Decision Making" (July 2012) http://www.bis.gov.uk/assets/biscore/business-law/docs/k/12–917-kay-review-of-equity-markets-final-report.pdf (accessed 5 March 2014).
4. http://www.publications.parliament.uk/pa/cm201213/cmselect/cmbis/uc969-ii/uc96901.htm (accessed 5 May 2014).
5. The Law Commission Fiduciary Duties of Investment Intermediaries: Initial Questions; Lord Cairns LC in *Parker v McKenna* (1874) LR 10 Ch App 96, at 118.
6. http://www.telegraph.co.uk/finance/newsbysector/banksandfinance/10676908/Barclays-We-paid-bonuses-to-avoid-death-spiral.html (accessed 5 March 2013).
7. http://europa.eu/rapid/press-release_STATEMENT-14–124_En.htm (accessed 3 May 2014).
8. http://ec.europa.eu/internal_market/accounting/non-financial_reporting/index_En.htm (accessed 3 May 2014).
9. http://www.theguardian.com/business/2014/mar/04/bankers-bonus-cap-architect-says-sue-uk-government (accessed 3 May 2014).
10. R. Higginson and D. Clough (2010) *Ethics of Executive Remuneration: A Guide for Christian Investors* (London: Church Investors Group).
11. https://www.frc.org.uk/Our-Work/Publications/Corporate-Governance/UK-Stewardship-Code-September-2012.pdf (accessed 5 March 2014).
12. The Large and Medium-sized Companies and Groups (Accounts and Reports) (Amendment) Regulations 2013.

13. http://www.bp.com/content/dam/bp/pdf/investors/directors_remuneration_report_2014.pdf (accessed 26 February 2014).
14. http://www.bp.com/content/dam/bp/pdf/investors/BP_Annual_Report_and_Accounts_200.pdf (accessed 26 February 2014).

8 The State and Tax

1. http://www.taxresearch.org.uk/Blog/2010/12/17/the-ethics-of-tax-avoidance/ (accessed 19 March 2014).
2. M. Porter (1990) *Competitive Advantage of Nations* (New York: Free Press).
3. http://www.oecd-library.org/docserver/download/5kg3h0vmd4kj.pdf?expires=1399374373&id=id&accname=guest&checksum=B998AF005F16EC6DAE3AC678B2BEF4A3 (accessed 6 May 2014).
4. http://www.nytimes.com/2012/12/02/us/how-local-taxpayers-bankroll-corporations.html?ref=louisestory (accessed 27 March 2012).
5. www.econlib.org/library/Enc1/ProgressiveTaxes.html (accessed 5 May 2014).
6. Ronald M. Green (1984) 'Ethics and Taxation', *The Journal of Religious Ethics*, 12, 2. pp 146–161.
7. http://www.telegraph.co.uk/news/worldnews/northamerica/usa/10731390/Why-Americas-poisonous-politics-makes-Market-Leninism-an-attractive-alternative.html (accessed 30 March 2014).
8. Consolidated Texts of the EU Treaties as Amended by the Treaty of Lisbon
9. http://www.hmrc.gov.uk/manuals/vexpmanual/vexp70400.htm (accessed 18 May 2014)
10. Alice Marwick, "Social Media's Broken Promise" New Scientist, 10 May 2014.
11. http://www.cadc.uscourts.gov/internet/opinions.nsf/F80DD179A16F848285257BA3004EA6D1/$file/12-1058-1445657.pdf (accessed 7 May 2014).
12. http://www.churchofengland.org/media/36534/gambling.pdf (accessed 7 May 2014).
13. Diocese of St Asaph, 29 April 2014.
14. Green, *Good Value*.

10 Ethical Frameworks and Case Studies

1. http://www.telegraph.co.uk/culture/books/bookreviews/10816161/Capital-in-the-Twenty-First-Century-by-Thomas-Piketty-review.html (accessed 11 May 2014).

Bibliography

M. Abrahamson (2009) *Conflicts of Interest in Investment Banking* (unpublished D.Phil. thesis, University of Oxford).

G.A. Aragon (2011) *Financial Ethics: A Positivist Analysis* (New York: Oxford University Press).

P. Arestis, R. Sobreira, and J.L. Oreiro (2011) *The Financial Crisis: Origins and Implications* (Basingstoke and New York: Palgrave Macmillan).

P. Arestis, R. Sobreira and J.L. Oreiro (2011a) *An Assessment of the Global Impact of the Financial Crisis* (Basingstoke: Palgrave Macmillan).

R. Audi (2009) *Business Ethics and Ethical Business* (New York and Oxford: Oxford University Press).

M. Ayub (2007) *Understanding Islamic Finance* (Chichester: Wiley).

E. Banks (2010) *See No Evil: Uncovering the Truth behind the Financial Crisis* (Basingstoke: Palgrave Macmillan).

Benedict XVI (2009) *Caritas in Veritate*.

T. Besley and P. Hennessy (2009) Letter to HM Queen Elizabeth II, 22 July 2009, following the British Academy Forum "The Global Financial Crisis – Why Didn't Anybody Notice?"

S. Bibb (2010) *The Right Thing to Do: An Everyday Guide to Ethics in Business* (Chichester: Wiley).

S. Bibb and J. Kourdi (2007) *A Question of Trust: The Crucial Nature of Trust in Business, Work and Life and How to Build It* (London: Cyan).

S. Blackburn (2001) *Being Good: An Introduction to Ethics* (Oxford: Oxford University Press).

J.R. Boatright (2010), *Finance Ethics: Critical Issues in Theory and Practice* (Hoboken, NJ: Wiley).

R. Bootle (2009) *The Trouble with Markets* (London and Boston: Nicholas Brealey Publishing).

R. Bradburn (2001) *Understanding Business Ethics* (London and New York: Continuum).

R. Brealey and S. Myers (2013) *Principles of Corporate Finance*, Global Edition (New York: McGraw Hill Higher Education).

G. Brown (2010) *Beyond the Crash: Overcoming the First Crisis of Globalisation* (London: Simon & Schuster).

A. Buckley (2011) *Financial Crisis: Causes, Context and Consequences* (Harlow and New York: Financial Times/Prentice Hall).

C. Cassell, P. Johnson and K. Smith (1997) "Opening the Black Box: Corporate Codes of ethics in their Organisational Context," *Journal of Business Ethics*, 16, 1077–93.

S.K. Chakraborty (1996) *Ethics in Management: Vedantic Perspectives* (Delhi: Oxford University Press).

A.Y.S. Chen, R.B. Sawyers and P.F. Williams (1997) "Reinforcing Ethical Decision Making through Corporate Culture," *Journal of Business Ethics*, 16, 855–65.

J.M. Childs (2000) *Greed: Economics and Ethics in Conflict* (Minneapolis: Fortress Press).

P.M.J. Christie, I.W.G. Kwon, P.A. Stoeberl and R. Baumhart (2003) "A Cross-Cultural Comparison of Ethical Attitudes of Business Managers: India, Korea and the United States," *Journal of Business Ethics*, 46 (3) 263–87.

G. Chryssides and J.H. Kaler (1996) *Essentials of Business Ethics* (London: McGraw Hill).

M. T. Cicero, *De Oficiisi [On Duties]*, M. Griffin and E. Atkins (eds) (Cambridge and New York: Cambridge University Press).

G. Cohen (2008) *Rescuing Justice and Equality* (Harvard: Harvard University Press).

J. Collier (1995) "The Virtuous Organization," *Business Ethics: A European Review*, 4 (3) 143–49.

J.W. Collins (1994) "Is Business Ethics an Oxymoron?" *Business Horizons*, September–October, 1–8.

A. Crane and D. Matten (2010) *Business Ethics: Managing Corporate Citizenship and Sustainability in the Age of Globalization*, 3rd edn (Oxford: Oxford University Press).

A. Crockett (2003) *Conflicts of Interest in the Financial Services Industry: What Should We Do About Them?* (London: Centre for Economic Policy Research).

C. Crouch and D. Marquand (eds) (1993) *Ethics and Markets: Co-operation and Competition within Capitalist Economies* (Oxford: Blackwell).

H. Davies (2010) *The Financial Crisis: Who Is to Blame?* (Cambridge: Polity Press).

R.T. De George (1999) *Business Ethics*, 5th edn (Upper Saddle River, NJ: Prentice Hall).

J. Deigh (2010) *An Introduction to Ethics* (Cambridge: Cambridge University Press).

M. Desai (2012) *The Incentive Bubble* (Harvard Business Review March).

M. Dewatripont, J.C. Rochet, J. Tirole and K. Tribe (2010) *Balancing the Banks: Global Lessons from the Financial Crisis* (Princeton and Oxford: Princeton University Press).

N. Dobos, C. Barry and T.W.M. Pogge (eds) (2011) *Global Financial Crisis: The Ethical Issues* (Basingstoke: Palgrave Macmillan).

T. Donaldson (2008) "Hedge Fund Ethics," *Business Ethics Quarterly*, 18 (3) 405–16.

O.C. Ferrell, J. Fraedrich, and L. Ferrell (2002) *Business Ethics: Ethical Decision Making and Cases*, 5th edn (Boston, MA: Houghton Mifflin).

Financial Reporting Council (2012) *The UK Corporate Governance Code*.

Financial Services Authority (2009) Discussion Paper "Short-Selling."

C. Fisher and A. Lovell (2008) *Business Ethics and Values: Individual, Corporate and International Perspectives*, 3rd edn (Harlow: Financial Times/Prentice Hall).

Francis (2013) *Evangelii Gaudium*.

R. Frederick (ed.) (1999) *A Companion to Business Ethics* (Oxford: Blackwell).

J. Friedman (ed.) (2011) *What Caused the Financial Crisis* (Philadelphia: University of Pennsylvania Press).

F. Fukuyama (1996) *Trust: The Social Virtues and the Creation of Prosperity* (London: Penguin).

J. Galbraith (1967) *The New Industrial State* (Princeton: Princeton University Press).

T. Geithner (2014) *Stress Test: Reflections on Financial Crises* (New York: Random House Publishing).

K. Gibson (2007) *Ethics and Business: An Introduction* (Cambridge: Cambridge University Press).

Goldman Sachs (2009) *Code of Business Conduct and Ethics*.

C.A.E. Goodhart (2009) *The Regulatory Response to the Financial Crisis* (Cheltenham and Northampton, MA: Edward Elgar).

R. M. Green (1984) "Ethics and Taxation," *The Journal of Religious Ethics*, 12 (2) pp 146–161.

R.M. Green (1994) *The Ethical Manager: A New Method for Business Ethics* (Eaglewood, NJ: Palgrave Macmillan).

S. Green (2009) *Good Value: Reflections on Money, Morality and an Uncertain World* (London: Allen Lane).

B. Griffiths (1982) *Morality and the Market Place* (London: Hodder and Stoughton).

B. Griffiths (2001) *Capitalism, Morality and Markets* (London: Institute of Economic Affairs).

T. Griseri (2010) *Business Ethics* (London: Cengage Learning).

R. Harries (1995) *Questioning Belief* (London: SPCK).

Harvard Business School (2003) *Harvard Business Review on Corporate Ethics* (Cambridge, MA: Harvard Business School Press).

K. Hassan, and M. Lewis (eds) (2007) *Islamic Finance* (Cheltenham: Edward Elgar).

G. Hegel (1991) *Elements of the Philosophy of Right*, ed. A. Wood, trans H. Nisbet (Cambridge: Cambridge University Press).

S.K. Henn (2009) *Business Ethics: A Case Study Approach* (Hoboken, NJ: Wiley).

R. Higginson and D. Clough (2010) *Ethics of Executive Pay: A Christian Viewpoint* (Cambridge: Grove).

R. Higginson and D. Clough (2010) *The Ethics of Executive Remuneration: A Guide for Christian Investors* (London: Church Investors Group).

N. Higgs-Kleyn and D. Kapeliansis (1999) "The Role of Professional Codes in Regulating Ethical Conduct," *Journal of Business Ethics*, 19, 363–74.

A. Hill (1998) *Just Business: Christian Ethics for the Market Place*, (Carlisle: Paternoster Press).

T. Hobbes, J. Gaskin (ed.) (1996) *Leviathan* (Oxford: Oxford University Press).

R. Hotten (2008) "Shell Plots $1.2 bn Regal Takeover Bid," *The Daily Telegraph*, 2 October.

S. Howes and P. Robins (1994) *A Theory of Moral Organization: A Buddhist View of Business Ethics* (Birmingham: Aston Business School Research Institute).

Independent Banking Commission (2010) *Issues Paper Call for Evidence*. http://webarchive.nationalarchives.gov.uk/20121204124254/http://bankingcommission.independent.gov.uk/wp-content/uploads/2010/07/issues-paper-24-september-2010.pdf (accessed 4 September 2014).

C. Jones, M. Parker and R. ten Bos (2005) *For Business Ethics: A Critical Approach* (London: Routledge).

I. Jones and M. Pollitt (eds) (1998) *The Role of Business Ethics in Economic Performance* (Basingstoke: Palgrave Macmillan).

D. Kahneman, (2011) *Thinking Fast and Slow* (London and New York: Allen Lane).

I. Kant (1970) *Kant's Political Writings*, H. Reiss (ed.) (Cambridge: Cambridge University Press).

I. Kant (1893) *Metaphysik der Sitten* (Berlin: Heimann).

J.M. Kline (2005) *Ethics for International Business: Decision Making in a Global Political Economy* (London: Routledge).

D. Koehn (1999) "What Can Eastern Philosophy Teach Us About Business Ethics?", *Journal of Business Ethics*, 19, 71–79.

R. Kolb (2006) *The Ethics of Executive Compensation* (Malden: Oxford and Carlton, Blackwell).

P. Koslowski (2011) *The Ethics of Banking: Conclusions from the Financial Crisis* (Dordrecht, Heildelberg, London, New York: Springer).

N.W. Leeson with E. Whitley (1997) *Rogue Trader* (London: Warner).

A. Levine (1980) *Free Enterprise and Jewish Law: Aspects of Jewish Business Ethics* (New York: Yeshiva University Press).

M. Lewis (2010) *The Big Short: Inside the Doomsday Machine* (London: Allen Lane).

M. Lewis (2014) *Flash Boys* (New York: W.W. Norton).

K.T. Liaw (2006) *The Business of Investment Banking: A Comprehensive Overview*, 2nd edn (Hoboken, NJ: Wiley).

J. Locke (2009) *Two Treatises On Government: A Translation Into Modern English* (ISR/Google Books).

J.L. Lynch (1994) *Banking and Finance: Managing the Moral Dimension* (Cambridge: Gresham/Woodhead).

A. MacIntrye (1984) *After Virtue: A Study in Moral Theory* (Notre Dame, Ill: University of Notre Dame Press).

K. Marx (2009) *Das Kapital* (Washington DC: Regenery Publishing).

A. Marwick (2014) *Status Update: Celebrity, Publicity and Branding in the Social Media Age* (New Haven and London: Yale University Press).

D.N. McCloskey (2006) *The Bourgeois Virtues: Ethics for an Age of Commerce* (Chicago: University of Chicago Press).

A.M. McCosh (1999) *Financial Ethics* (Boston, MA: Kluwer Academic Publishers).

T. McEwan (2001) *Managing Values and Beliefs in Organisations* (Harlow: Pearson Education).

C.W. McLemore (2003) *Street-Smart Ethics: Succeeding in Business without Selling Your Soul*, (Louisville and London: Westminster John Knox Press).

C. Megone and S. J. Robinson (eds) (2002) *Case Histories in Business Ethics* (London and New York: Routledge).

A. Meir (2009) *Jewish Values Based Investment Guide* (Jerusalem: Business Ethics Center of Jerusalem).

D. Melé (2009) *Business Ethics in Action* (Basingstoke: Palgrave Macmillan).

N. Messer (2006) *SCM Studyguide to Christian Ethics* (London: SCM).

C. Moon and C. Bonny (2001) *Business Ethics: Facing up to the Issues* (London: Economist Books).

D.A. Moore (ed.) (2005) *Conflicts of Interest: Challenges and Solutions in Business, Law, Medicine, and Public Policy* (Cambridge: Cambridge University Press).

G.E. Moore (1903) *Principia Ethica*. (Cambridge: Cambridge University Press).

J. Moore (1990) "What is really Unethical about Insider Trading?" *Journal of Business Ethics*, 9, 171–82.

D. Morris (2004) "Defining a Moral Problem in Business Ethics," *Journal of Business Ethics*, 49, 347–57.

A. Newton (1998) *Compliance: Making Ethics Work in Financial Services* (London: Pitman).

F. Nietzsche (1883) *Also Sprach Zarathrustra* (Chemnitz: Verlag von Ernst Schmeitzner).

R. Nozick (1974) *Anarchy, State and Utopia* (New York: Basic Books).

M.K. Nyaw and I. Ng (1994) "A Comparative Analysis of Ethical Beliefs: A Four Country Study," *Journal of Business Ethics*, 13 (7) 543–55.

J. Oakley and D. Cocking (2001) *Virtue Ethics and Professional Roles* (Cambridge: Cambridge University Press).

T. O'Brien and S. Paeth (eds) (2007) *Religious Perspectives on Business Ethics: An Anthology* (Lanham, MD and Plymouth: Rowman & Littlefield).

O. O'Neill (2002) *A Question of Trust* (Cambridge: Cambridge University Press).

A.R. Paley and D.S. Hilzenrath (2008) "SEC Chief Defends His Restraint" *Washington Post*, 24 November, http://www.washingtonpost.com/wp-dyn/content/article/2008/12/23/AR2008122302765.html (accessed 8 March 2011).

M.L. Pava (1998) "The Substance of Jewish Business Ethics," *Journal of Business Ethics*, 17 (6) 603–17.

T. Piketty (2014) *Capital in the Twenty First Century* (Harvard: Harvard University Press).

M. Porter (1990) *The Competitive Advantage of Nations* (New York: Free Press).

S.R. Premeaux and R.W. Mondy (1993) "Linking Management Behavior to Ethical Philosophy," *Journal of Business Ethics*, 12, 349–57.

A. Rand (1992) *Atlas Shrugged 35th Anniversary Edition* (New York: Dutton).

A. Rand (1967) *Capitalism, the Unknown Ideal* (New York: New American Library).

J. Rawls (1971) *A Theory of Justice* (Cambridge, MA: Harvard University Press).

J. Reynolds (2010) "Investment Banking: The Inevitable Triumph of Incentives over Ethics" in R. Williams and L. Elliott (eds) *Crisis and Recovery* (Basingstoke: Palgrave Macmillan).

J. Reynolds and E. Newell (2012) *Ethics in Investment Banking* (Basingstoke: Palgrave Macmillan).

B. Rider, K. Alexander and L. Linklater (2007) *Market Abuse and Insider Dealing* (Haywards Heath: Tottel).

S.B. Rosenthal and R.A. Buchholz (2000) *Rethinking Business Ethics: A Pragmatic Approach* (New York and Oxford: Oxford University Press).

J-J. Rousseau *Du contrat social ou Principes du droit politique* (1762).

D.A. Sabalot (2013) *Butterworths Securities and Financial Services Law Handbook* (London: Butterworths Law).

A.H.M. Sadeq and K. Ahmad (eds) (2001) *Ethics in Business and Management: Islamic and Mainstream Approaches* (London: Asean Academic).

M. Schwartz (2000) "Why Ethical Codes Constitute an Unconscionable Regression," *Journal of Business Ethics*, 23, 173–84.

A. Seldon (2009) *Trust: How We Lost it and How to Get it Back* (London: Biteback).

P. Singer (ed.) (1991) *A Companion to Ethics* (Oxford: Blackwell).

H.W. Sinn (2010) *Casino Capitalism: How the Financial Crisis Came About and What Needs to be Done Now* (Oxford: Oxford University Press).

A. Smith (1759) *The Theory of Moral Sentiments*. (London: A. Millar).

A. Smith (1776) *The Wealth of Nations* (London: W. Strahan and T. Cadell).

A. R. Sorkin (2014) *What Timothy Geithner Really Thinks* (New York: New York Times, 8 May 2014).

A.R. Sorkin (2009) *Too Big to Fail: The Inside Story of How Wall Street and Washington Fought to Save the Financial System from Crisis – and Themselves* (New York: Viking).

M.L. Stackhouse (2001) "Business, Economics and Christian Ethics" in R. Gill (ed.) *The Cambridge Companion to Christian Ethics* (Cambridge: Cambridge University Press).

M.L. Stackhouse, D.P. McCann, S.J. Roels, with P.N. Williams (1995) *On Moral Business: Classical and Contemporary Resources for Ethics in Economic Life* (Grand Rapids, MI: Eerdmans).

P.A. Stanwick, and S.D. Stanwick (2009) *Understanding Business Ethics* (Upper Saddle River, NJ: Pearson/Prentice Hall).

E. Sternberg (2000) *Just Business: Business Ethics in Action*, 2nd edn (Oxford: Oxford University Press).

J.E. Stiglitz (2010) *Freefall: Free Markets and the Sinking of the Global Economy* (London: Penguin).

S. Strange (1986) *Casino Capitalism* (Oxford: Blackwell).

R. Sullivan (ed.) (2003) *Business and Human Rights: Dilemmas and Solutions* (Sheffield: Greenleaf).

M.P. Taylor and R.H. Clarida (2011) *The Global Financial Crisis* (London: Routledge).

W. Temple (1984) *Christianity and Social Order* (London: Shepheard-Walwyn, New Edition 1984).

S. Thomsen, C. Rose and O. Risager (2009) *Understanding the Financial Crisis: Investment, Risk and Governance* (Copenhagen: SimCorp).

P. Ulrich, (2008) *Integrative Economic Ethics: Foundations of a Civilized Market Economy* (Cambridge: Cambridge University Press).

K.C. van Cranenburgh, D. Arenas, C. Louche and J. Vives (2010) *From Faith to Faith Consistent Investing* (Barcelona: 3iG).

M.G. Velasquez (1998) *Business Ethics: Concepts and Cases*, 4th edn (Upper Saddle River, NJ: Prentice Hall).

J. Verstraeten (ed.) (2000) *Business Ethics: Broadening the Perspectives* (Leuven: Peters).

W.K.S. Wang and M.I. Steinberg (2010) *Insider Trading*, 3rd edn (New York and Oxford: Oxford University Press).

M. Weber *The Protestant Ethic and the Spirit of Capitalism* (USA: First Printing).

S. Webley (ed.) (2008) *Use of Codes of Ethics in Business: 2007 Survey and Analysis of Trends* (London: Institute of Business Ethics).

S. Webley and M. Le Jeune (2005) *Corporate Use of Codes of Ethics: 2004 Survey* (London: Institute of Business Ethics).

I. Wienen (1999) *Impact of Religion on Business Ethics in Europe and the Muslim World: Islamic versus Christian Tradition* (Oxford: Peter Lang).

R. Williams and L. Elliott (eds) (2010) *Crisis and Recovery* (Basingstoke: Palgrave Macmillan).

C. Wright (2004) *The Business of Virtue* (London: SPCK).

R. Younglai (2008) "SEC Chief has regrets over short-selling ban," 31 December http://www.reuters.com/article/2008/12/31/us-sec-cox-idUS-TRE4BU3GG20081231 (accessed 8 March 2011).

L. Zsolnai (2011) *Spirituality and Ethics in Management*, 2nd edn (Dordrecht, Hedielberg, London, New York: Springer).

Index